Pluck This

An A-to-Z Eyebrow Fantasia

Illustrations by
Julia Hartling
Text by
Melissa Markoff

Furrowed Brow Productions, L.L.C.
www.pluckthisbook.com

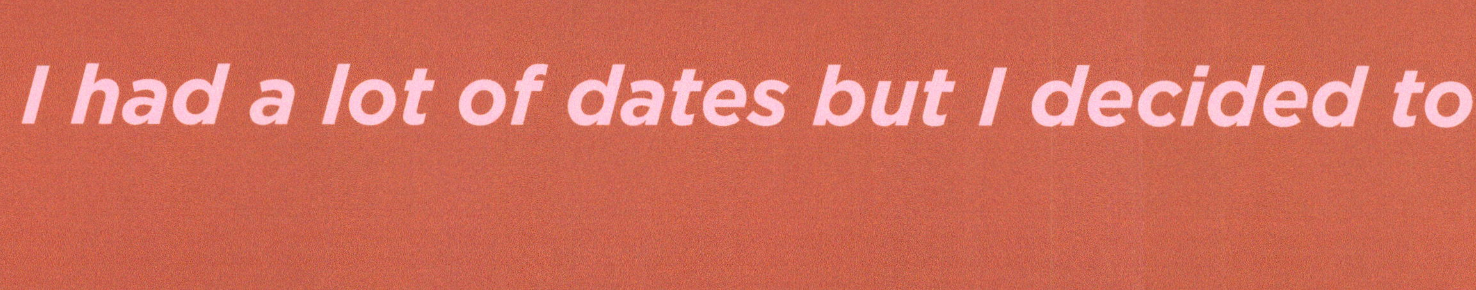
I had a lot of dates but I decided to

stay home and dye my eyebrows.

—Andy Warhol

This book would not have been possible without the help of Nicole Markoff, Tod Winston, Jonathan Glick, Janessa Post, Tom Salamon, Monique Peterson, Chester Rothstein, Will Frank, and Noah Markoff. Special thanks to Ilya and Jim for all their support.—**JH and MM**

Published by Furrowed Brow Productions, L.L.C.

ISBN 978-0-9969434-0-6

Contents

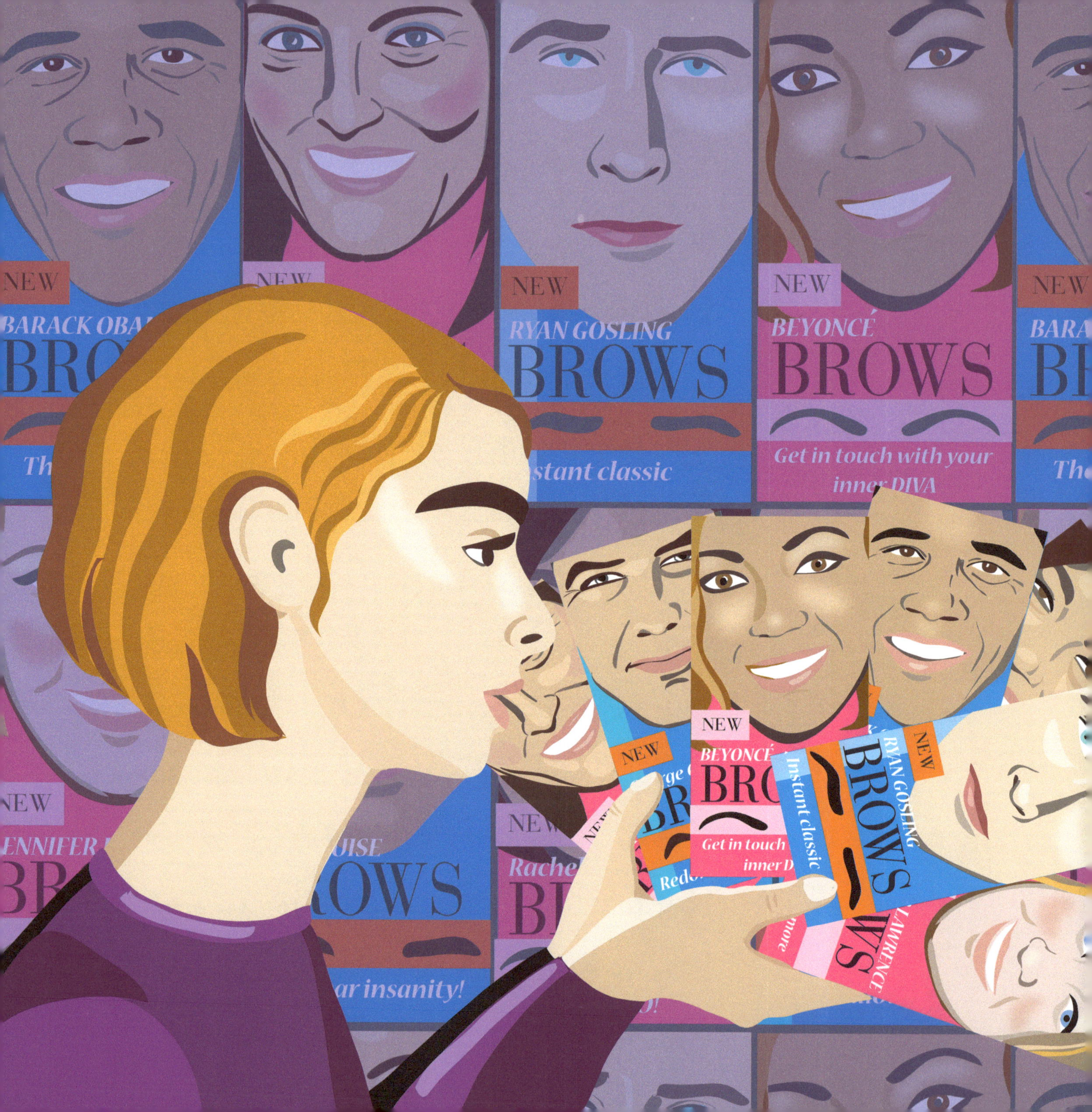
NEW
NEW
RYAN GOSLING
BROWS
NEW
BEYONCÉ
BROWS
Get in touch with your
inner DIVA
NEW
NEW
BEYONCÉ
NEW
RYAN GOSLING
BROWS
Instant classic
LAWRENCE

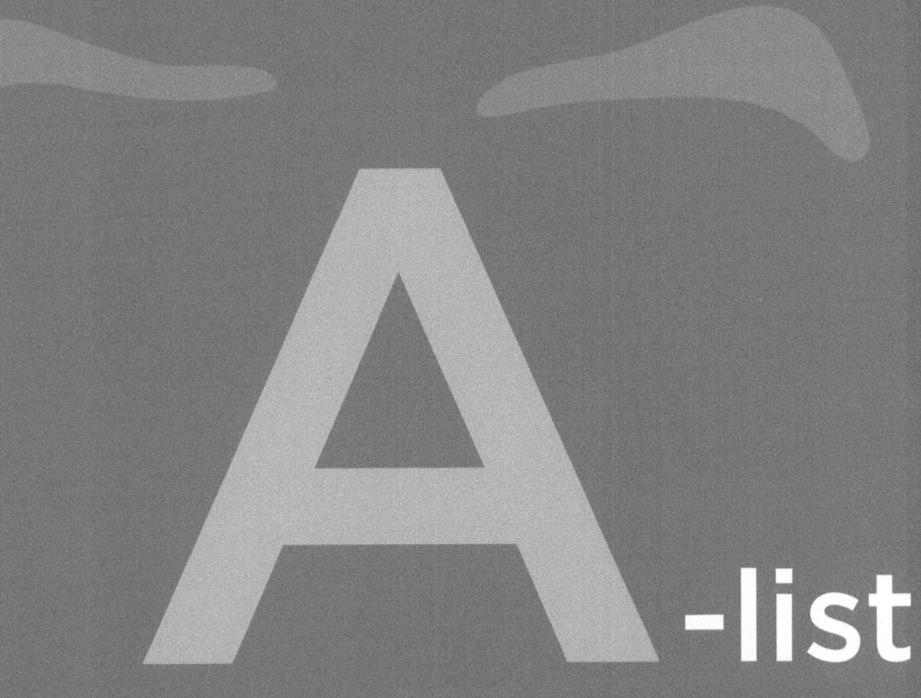

A-list

Are your brows super blah?
Go from “meh” to “totally wow!”
Grab an A-List Brow today—
Try Jay-Z or Rachael Ray...
Check you out! Who’s the fab one now?

Bling

B is for Bling Brows
Like diamonds in the sky
Tiny suns rise up your forehead
So bright, they'll make you cry.

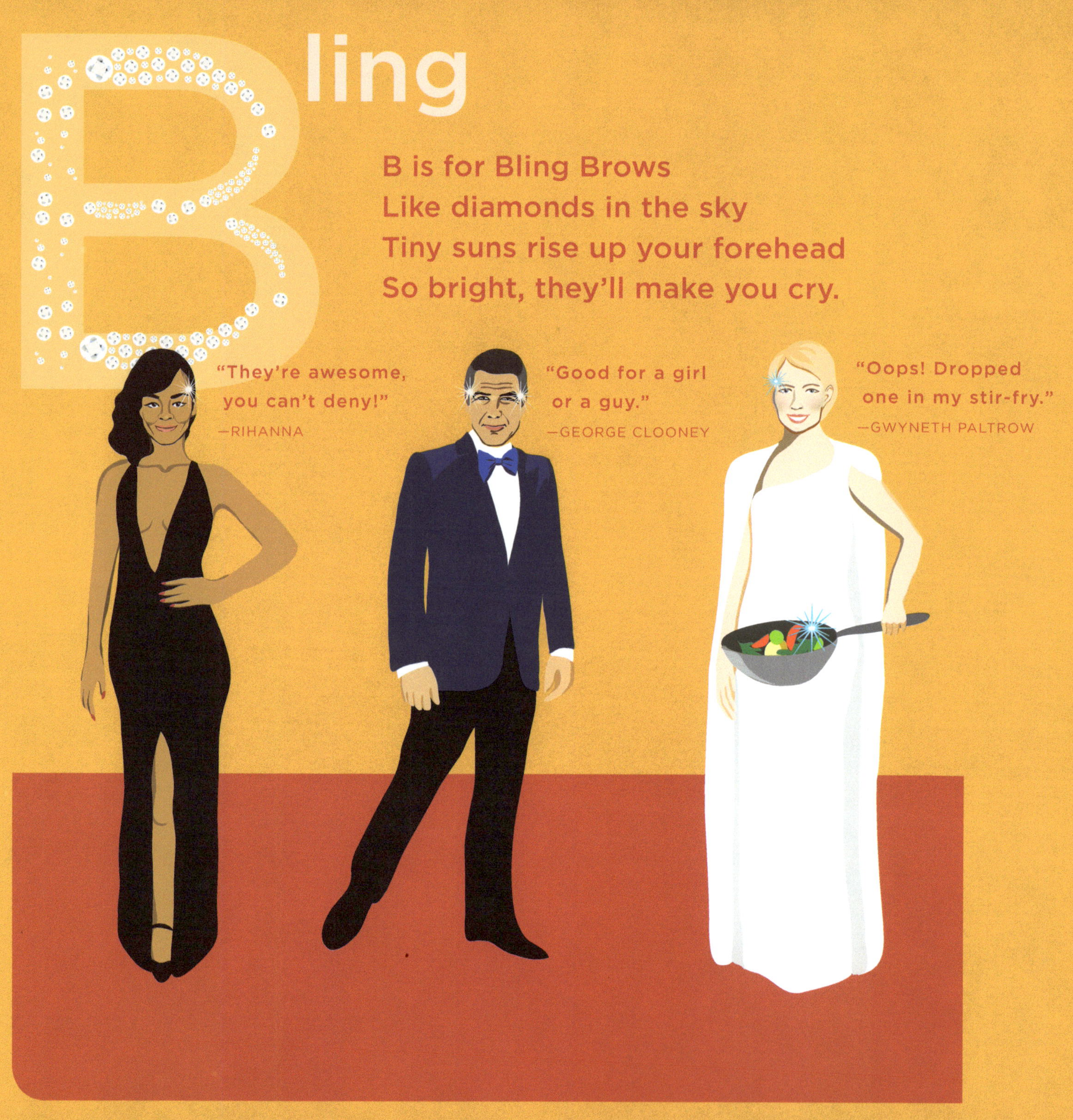

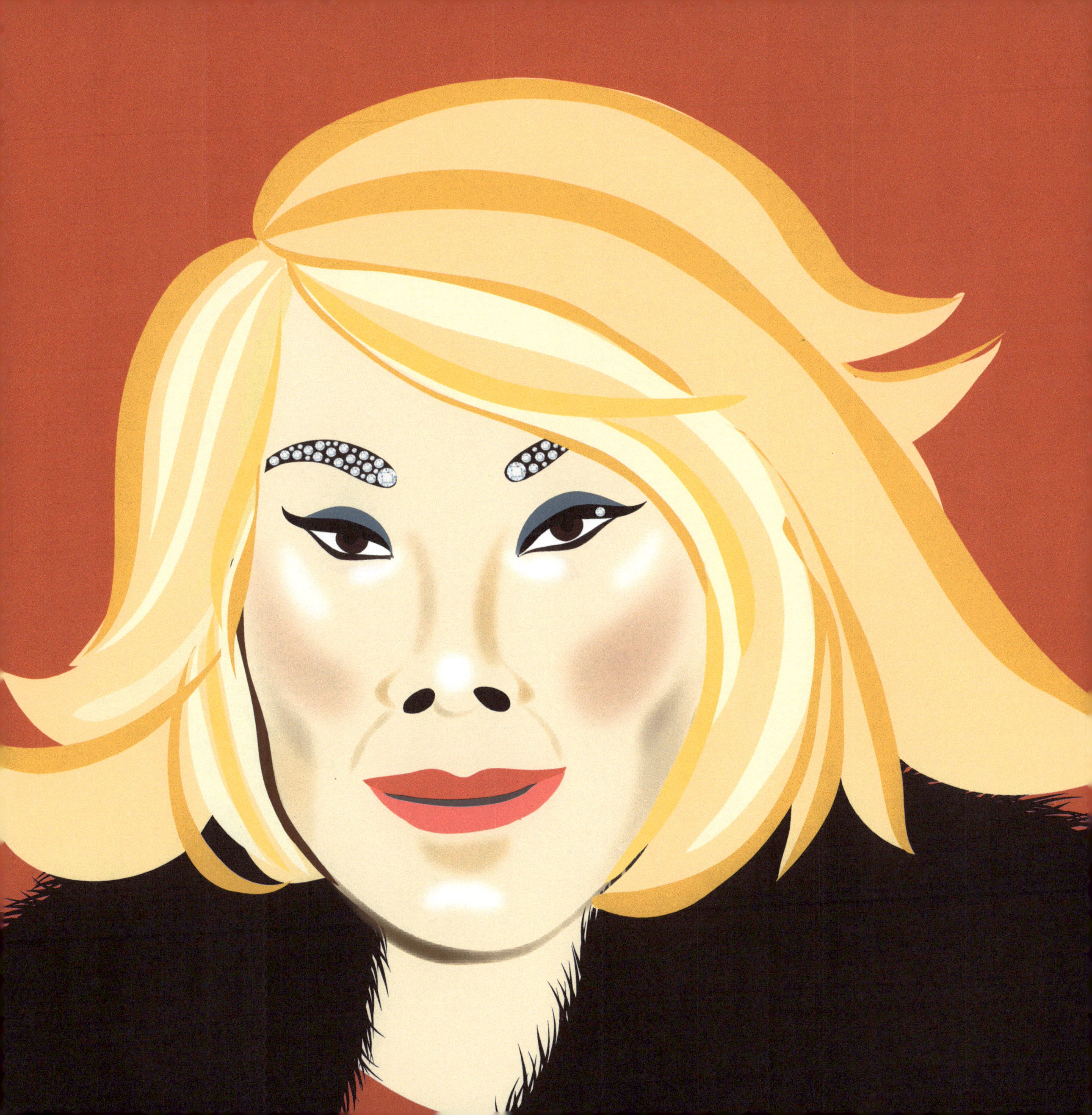

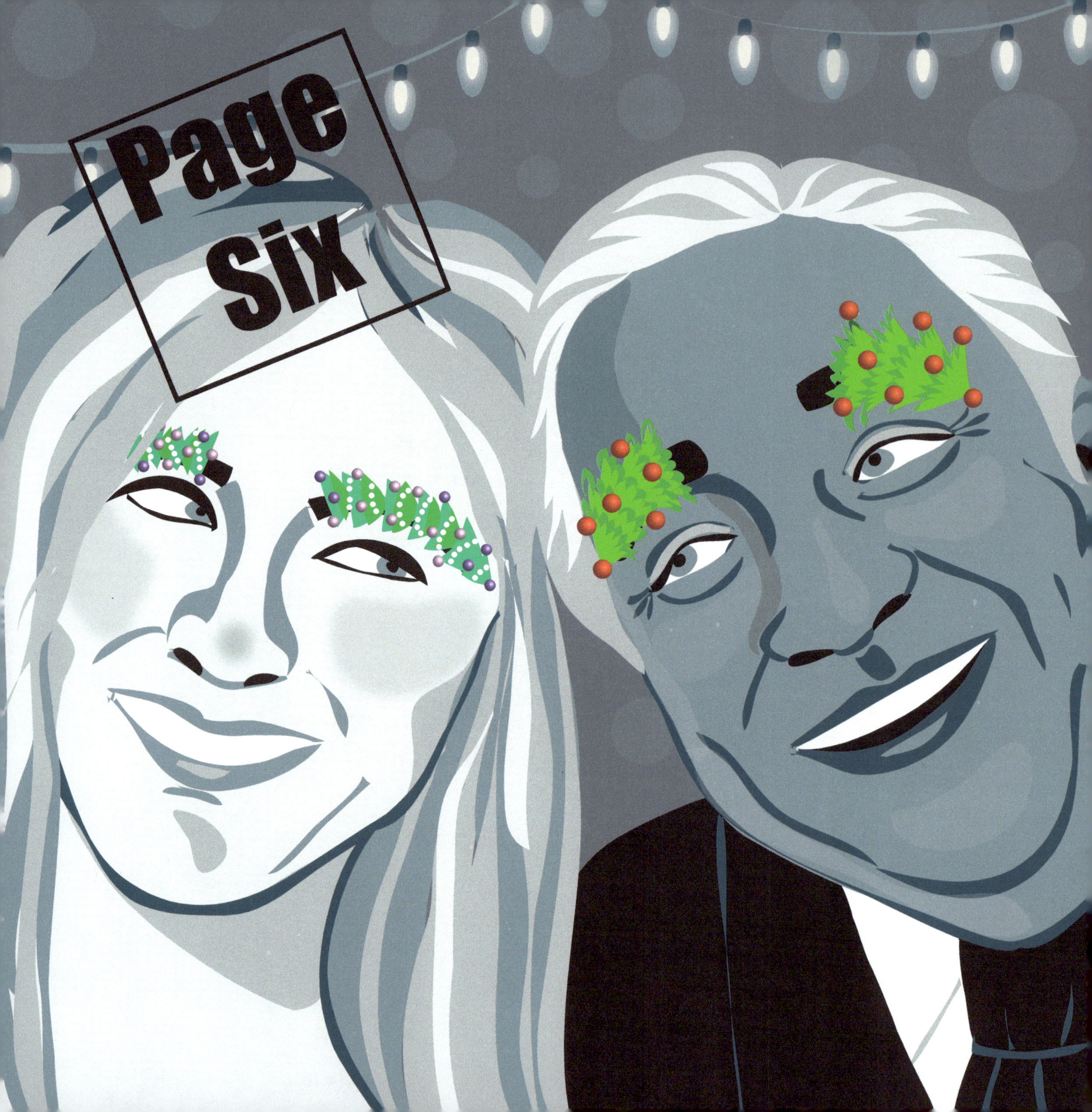
Page
Six

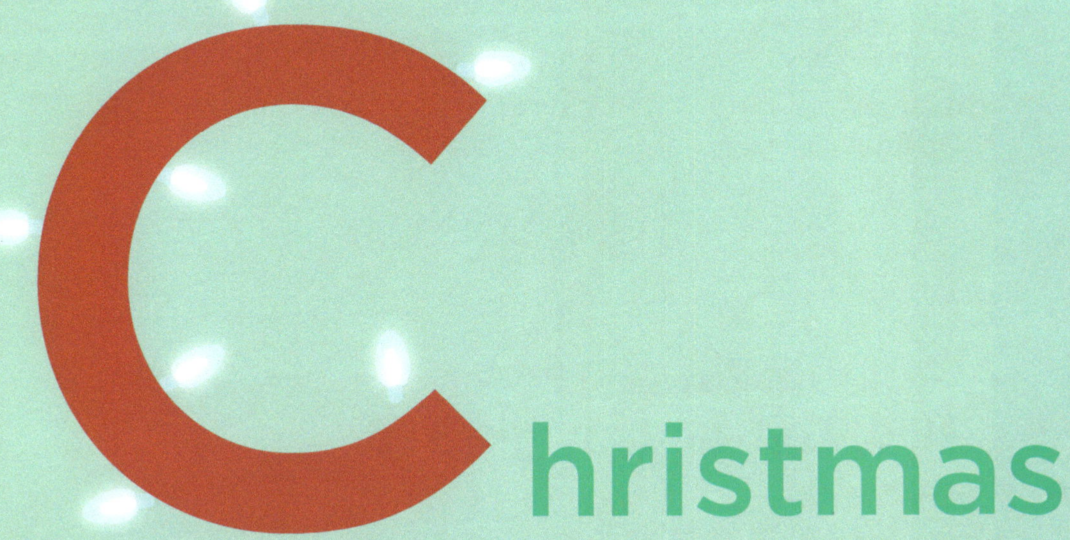

C is for Christmas Brows
With ornaments all a-dangle
They flatter all types of faces
From Jennifer Aniston to Charles Rangel.

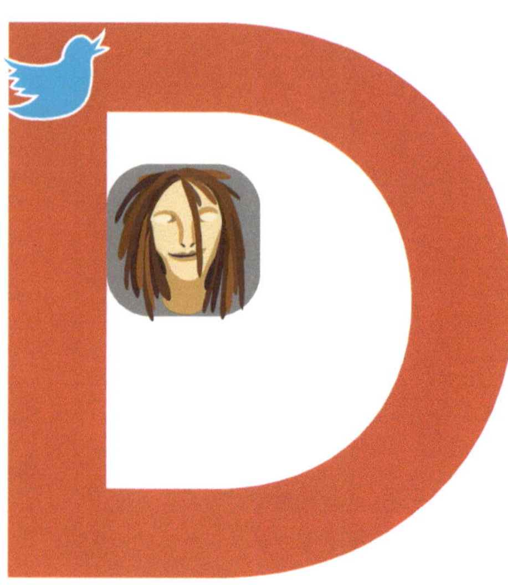

is for #Dreads

@lovingda90s

Grow 'em on brows instead of your head.

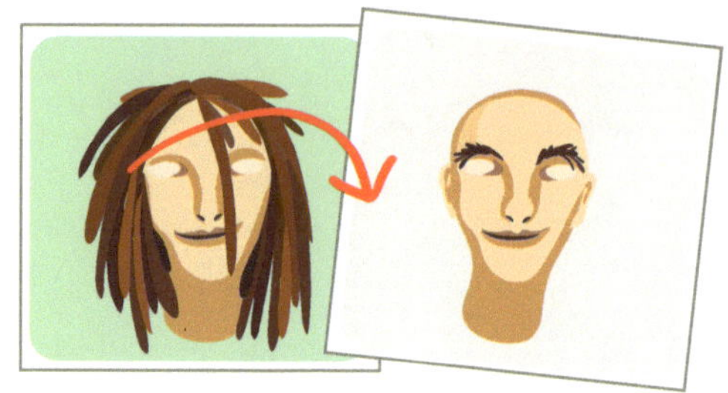

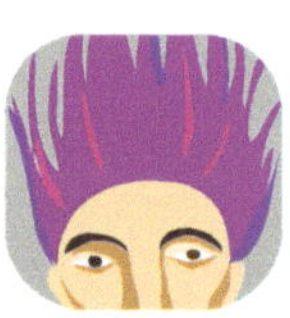

Troll Girl @bighairdollz

Ned, Zed, and my girl Ted.

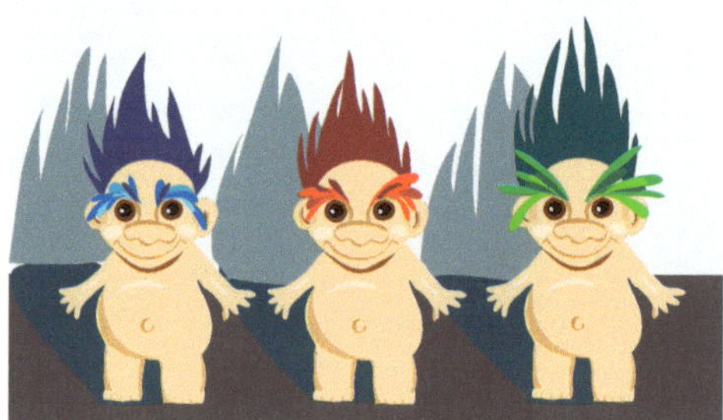

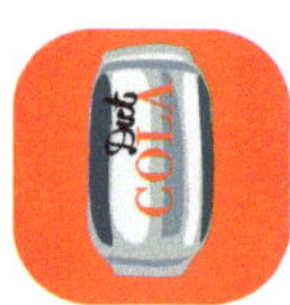

Diet Cola Luvah @DietColaLuvah

White and Red.

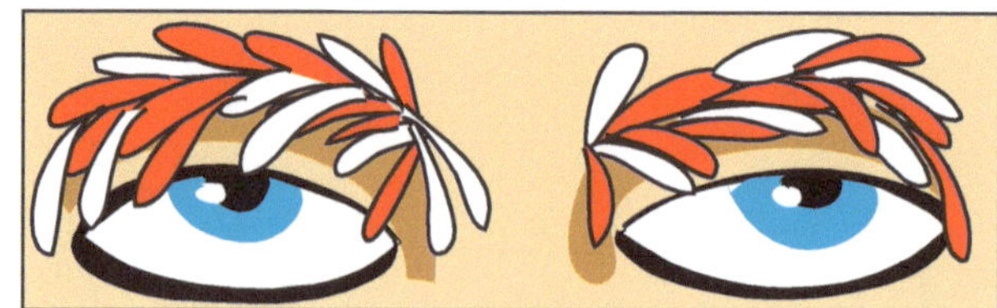

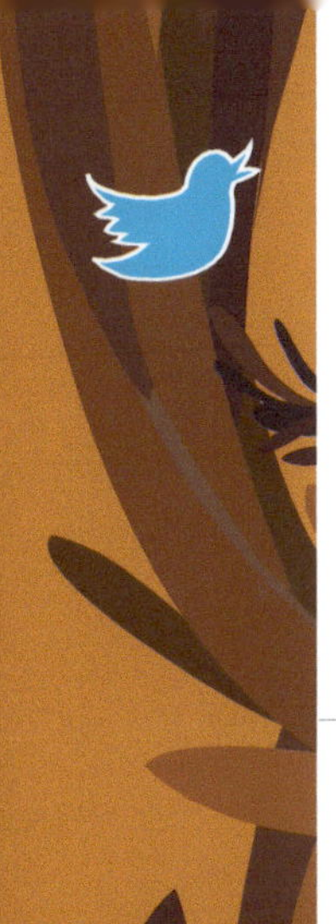

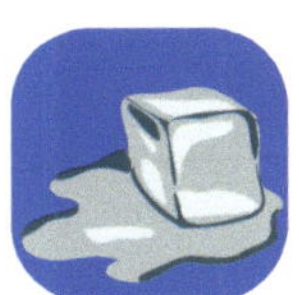

Ice Ice Baby @mixtape4ever

Street Cred.

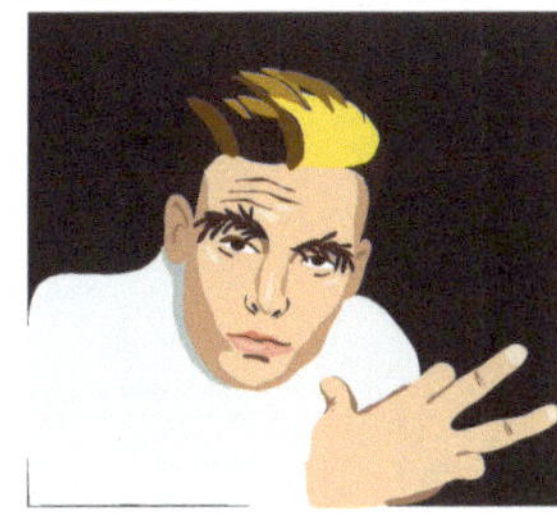

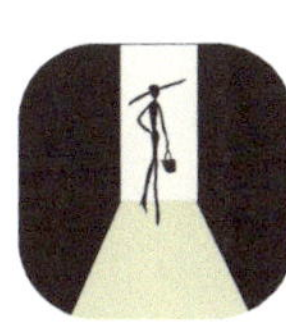

Catwalker @Im2sexyyo

Right Said Fred!

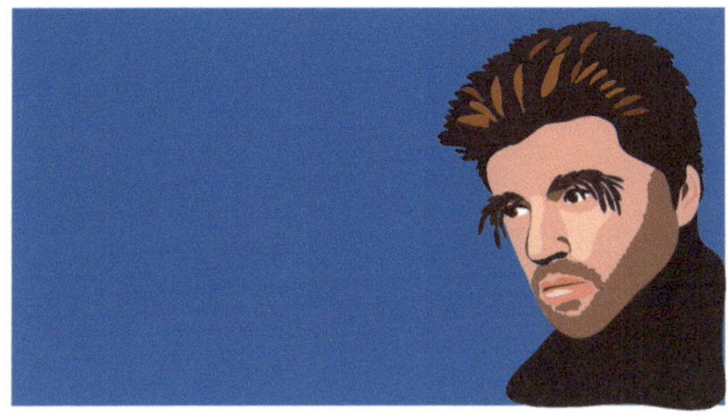

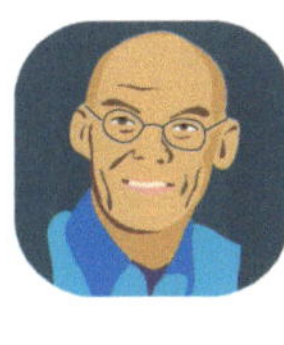

James @STILLtheeconomy

This style ain't dead!

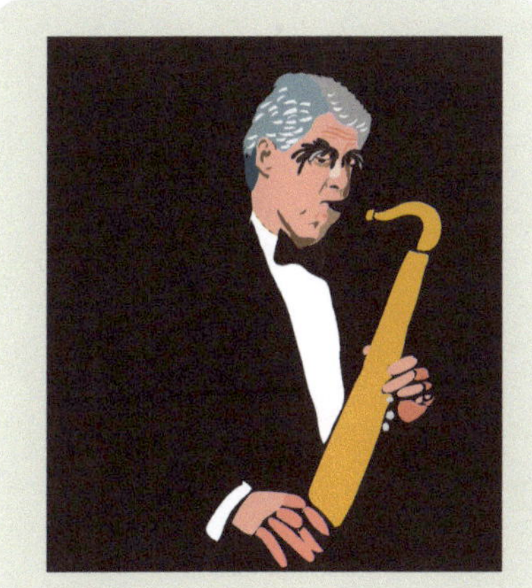

Elephant

When the world gets wind of your Elephant Brow
It'll spawn a media circus.
But soon all will grovel
'Cuz your brow's a novel
That just won rave reviews in *Kirkus*.

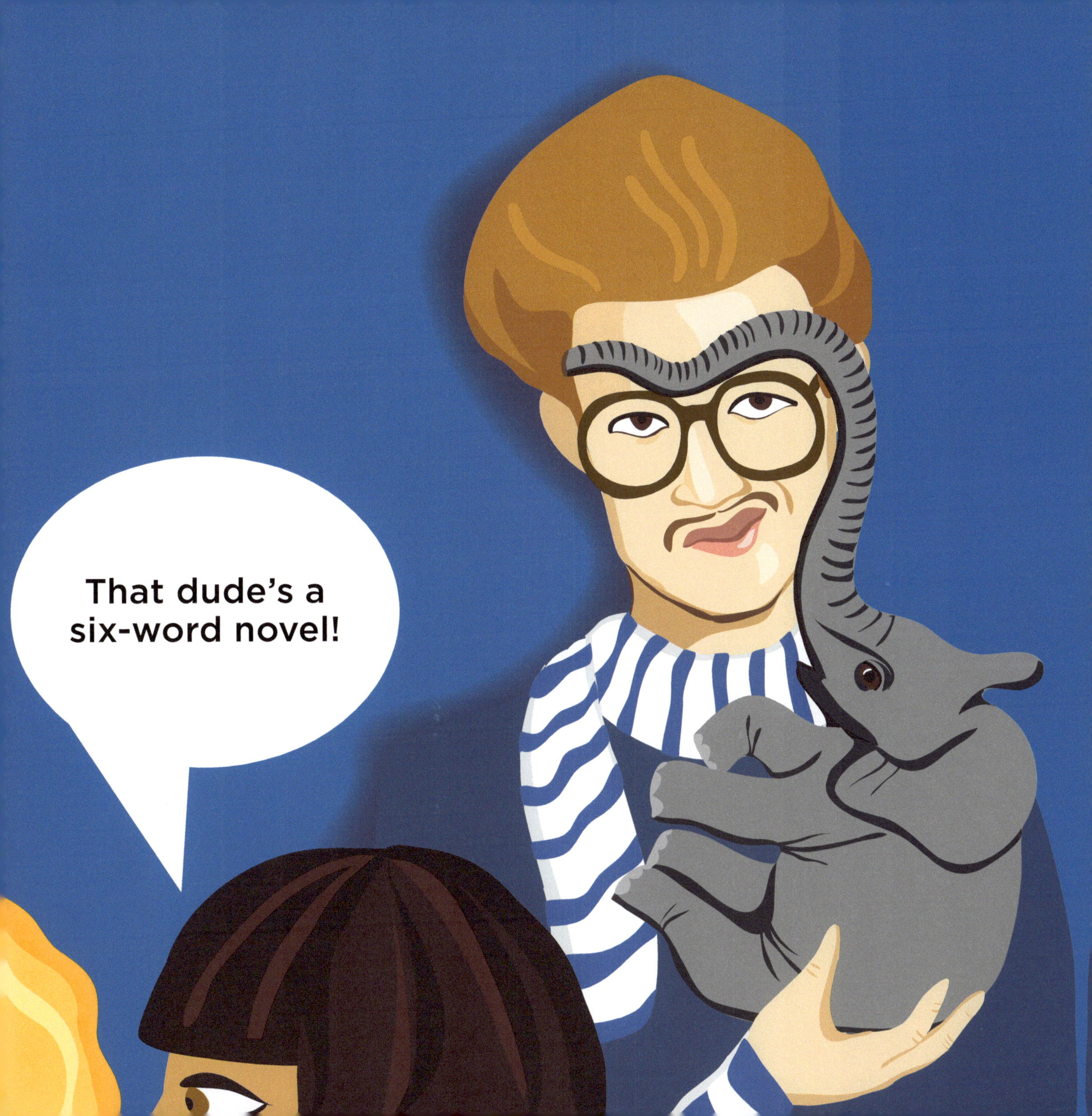
That dude's a
six-word novel!

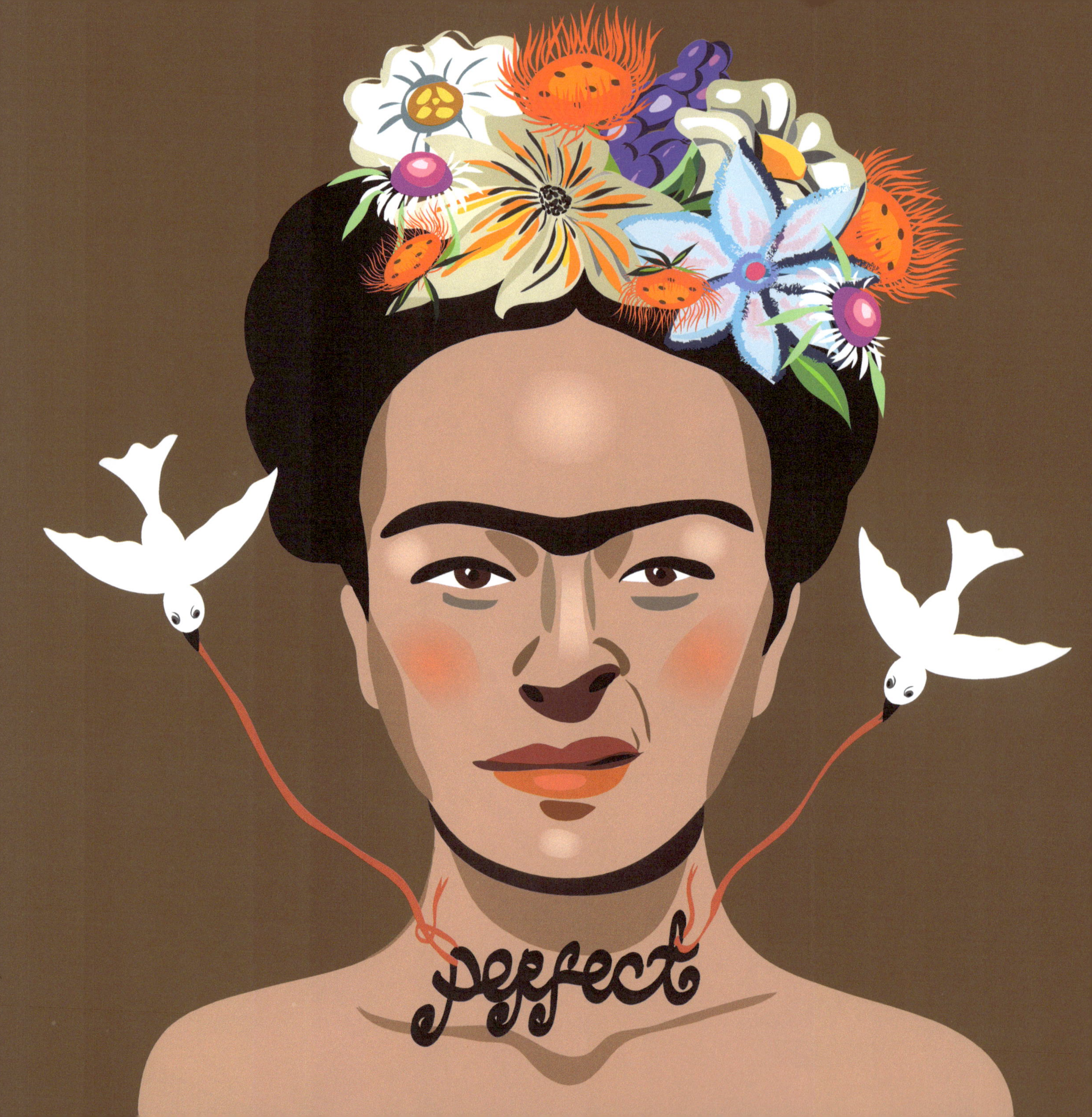
perfect

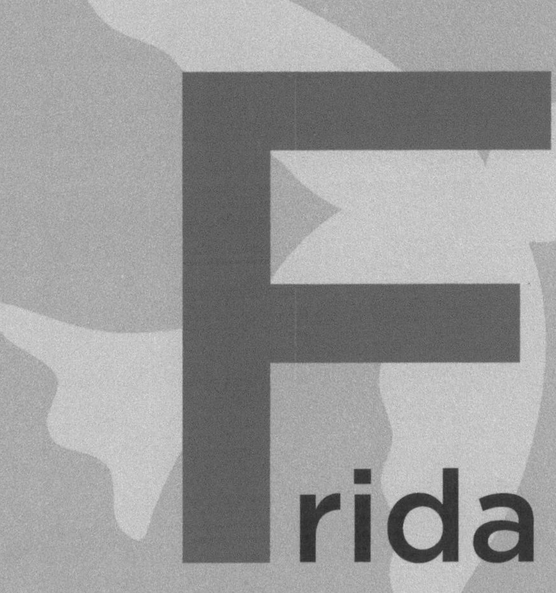

Frida

Frida looked in the mirror and said, “Fuck it!”
Her tweezer then she did chuck it
“My unibrow isn’t bad
It’s totally rad
So if you don’t like it, go suck it!”

Gertrude

An eyebrow is an eyebrow is an eyebrow,
Unless you're Picasso,
In which case, it's a hangnail.

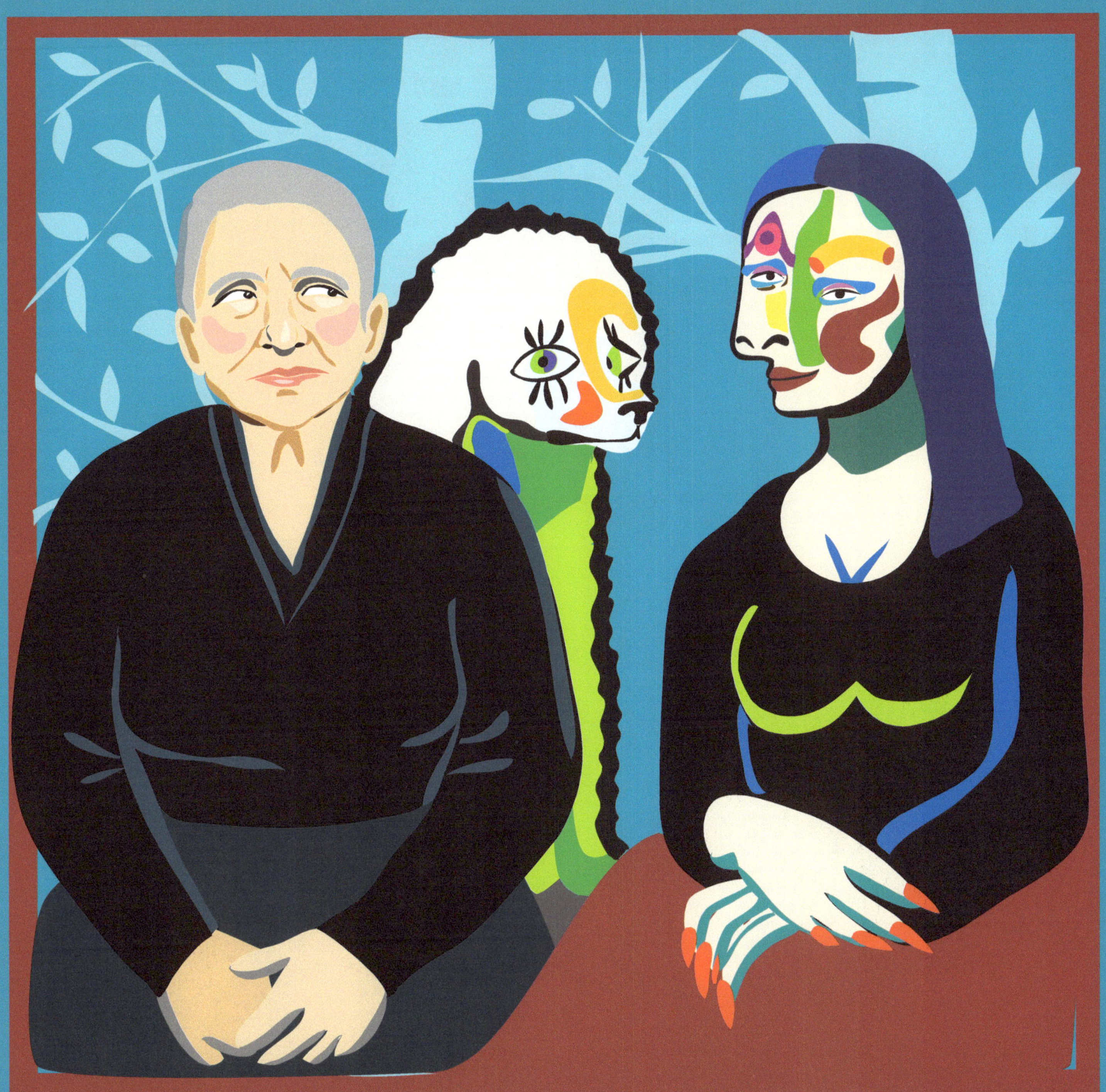

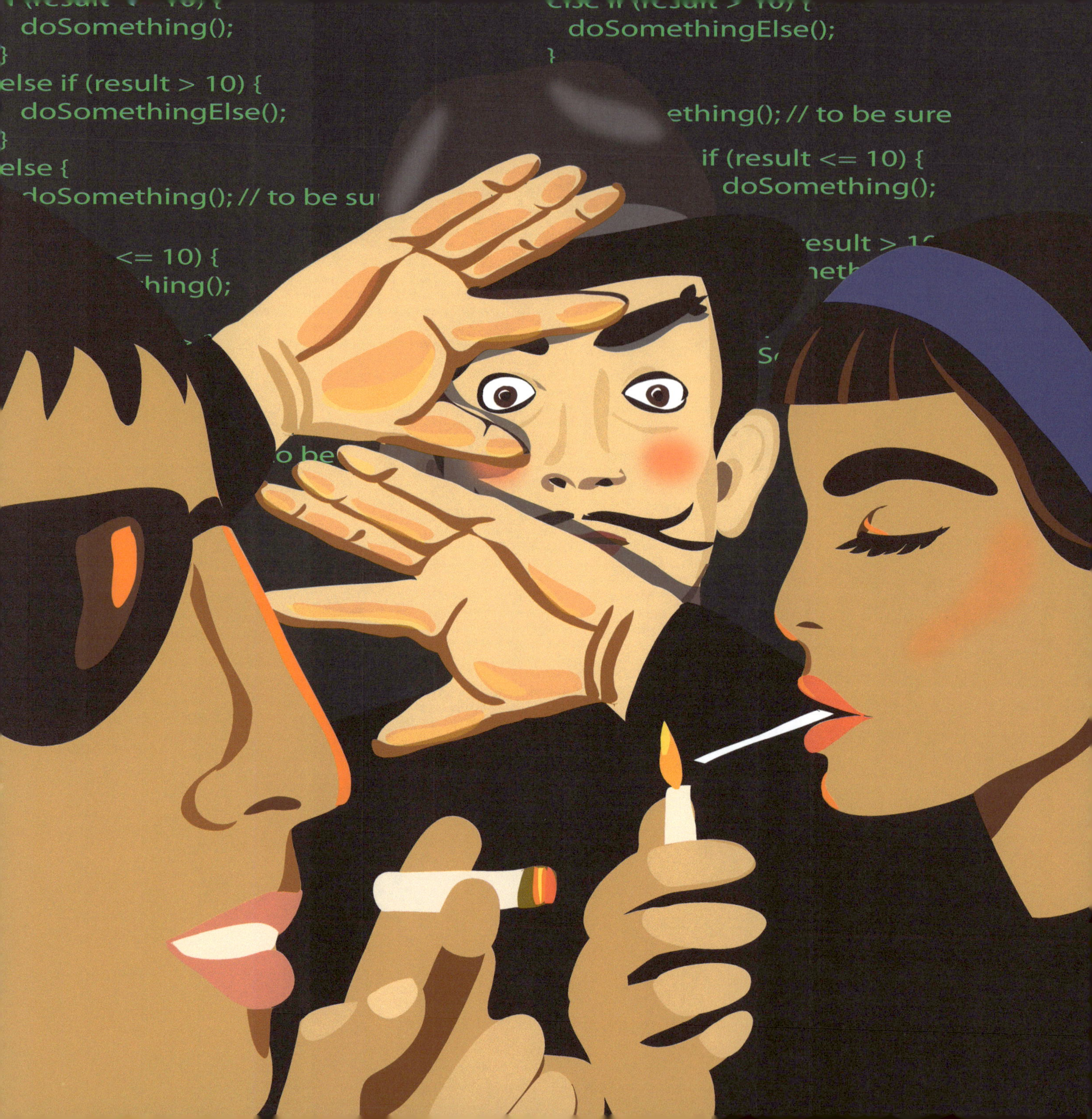

doSomething();
}
else if (result > 10) {
doSomethingElse();
}
else {
doSomethingElse();
}
ething(); // to be sure
if (result <= 10) {
doSomething();

Brogrammer's a crazy code-writer
And with his *Hindenburg* Brow, quite-a-sighter
But you do not want to explode
His hydrogen-filled node
So please, man, put down your lighter!

Hindenburg

Ivy League

O Ivy League Brow!
You're the coolest of the cool
Would you ever consider dating
A graduate of State U?

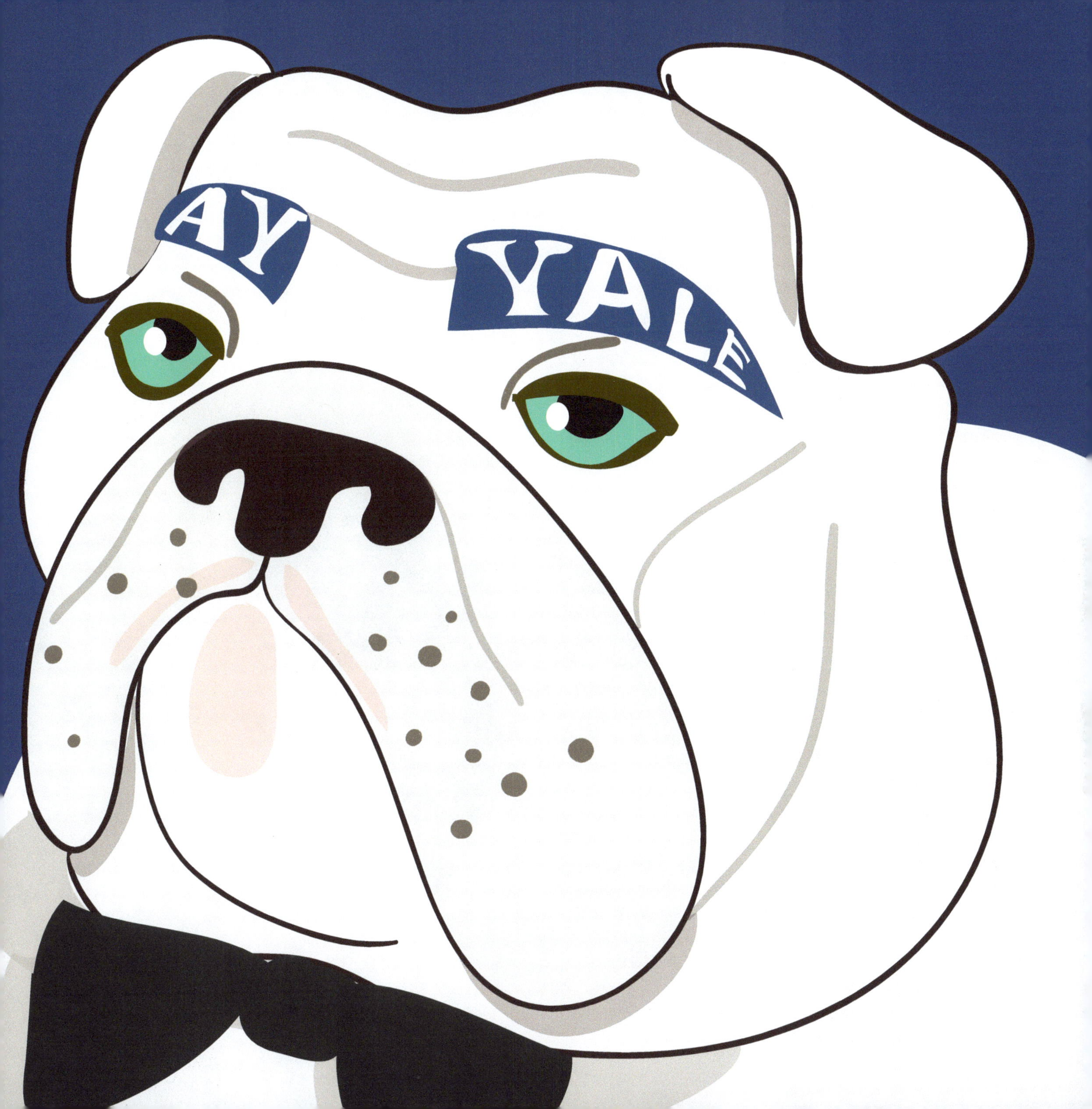
AY
YALE

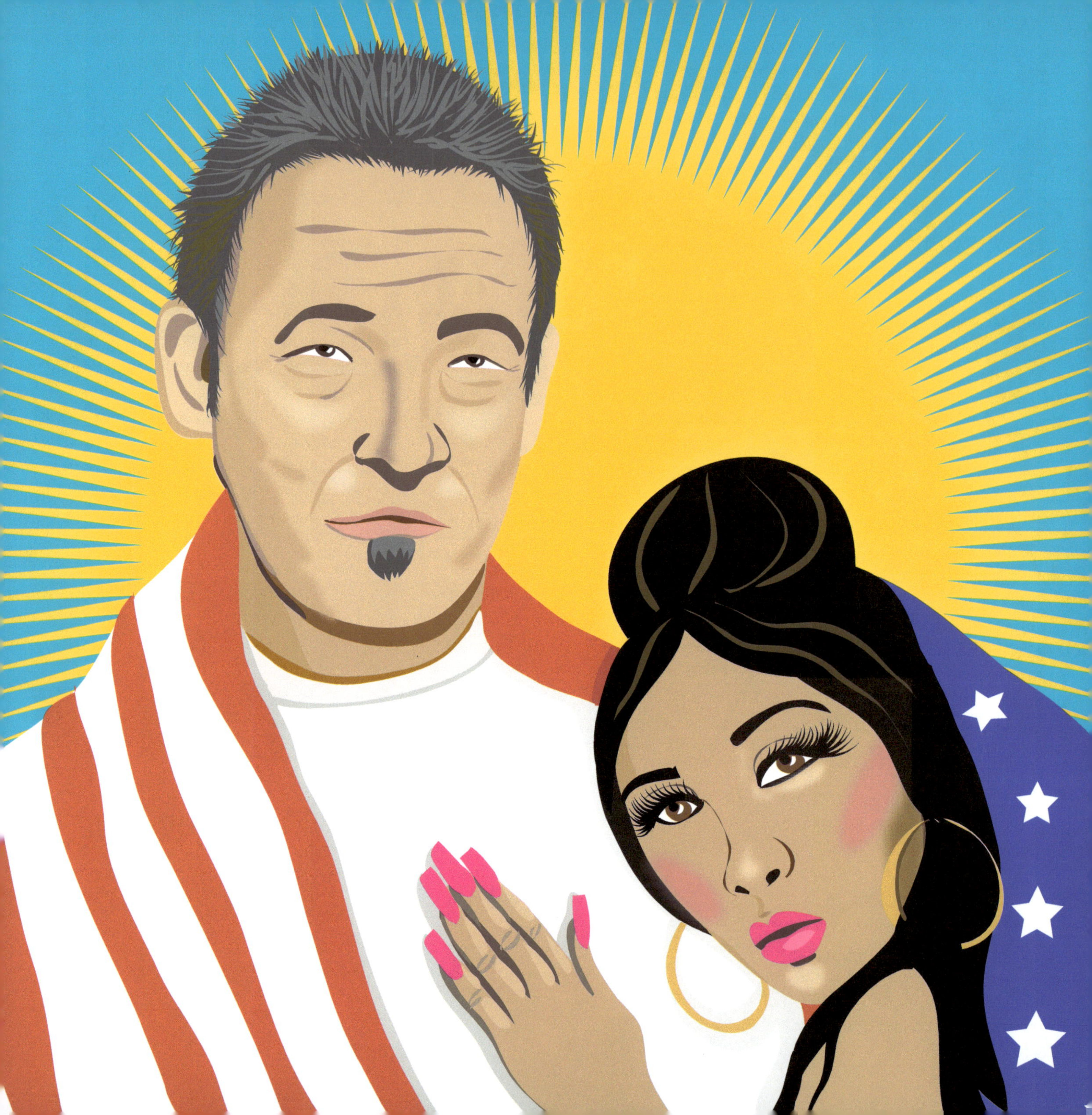

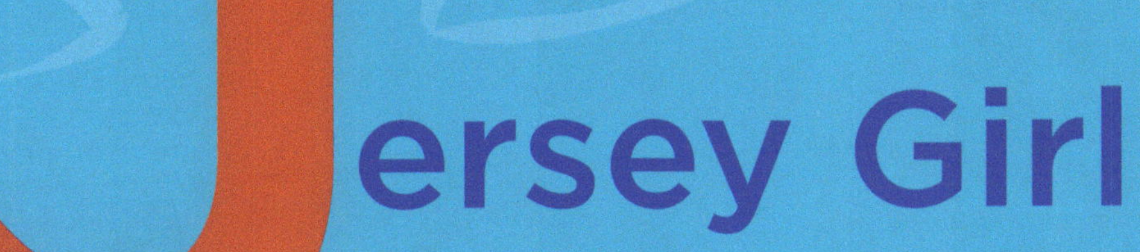

Jersey Girl

Gotta love the Jersey Girl's Brow!
So what if critics don't get it?
It's a brilliantly shellacked hair bump—
So cute, you just want to pet it!

Kansas

After a whirlwind tour of Oz
Dorothy returned to life on the plains
“Your Kansas Brow’s a great look!” Aunt Em said
“Amber waves of true heartland grains.”

“Better get over it, Em,
’Cuz I’m headin’ to the threader’s right now.
She’s gonna beat these bitches into submission;
I’m gettin’ a Marlene Dietrich-type brow!”

“Dorothy! Are you out of your gourd?
Mess with your image and dearly you’ll pay
History’s littered with rebranding failures
Remember New Coke and Jennifer Grey?

“Your Kansas brow is totally money
So for the love of God, don’t fuck with it, honey!”

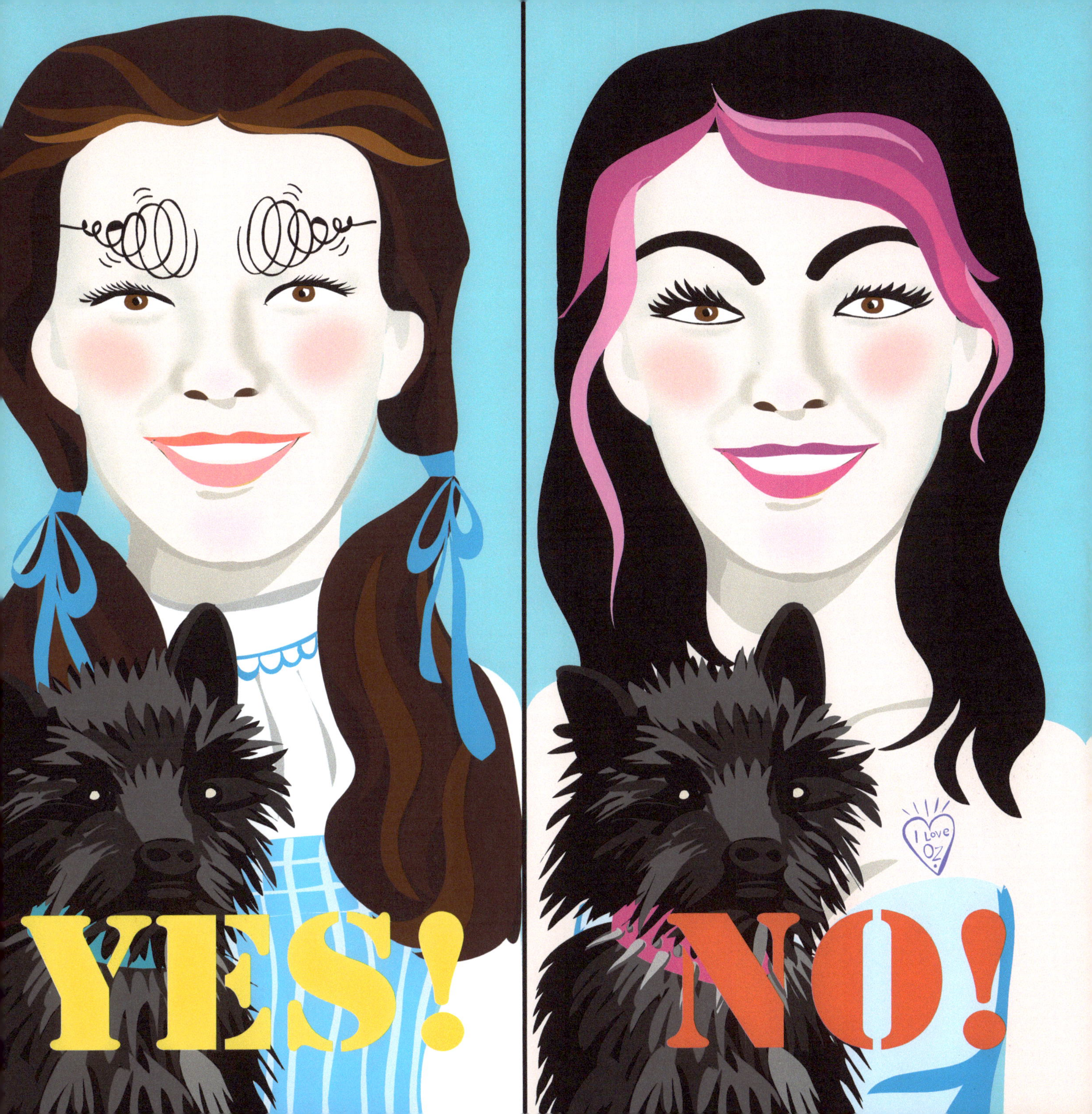
YES!
NO!
I Love OZ

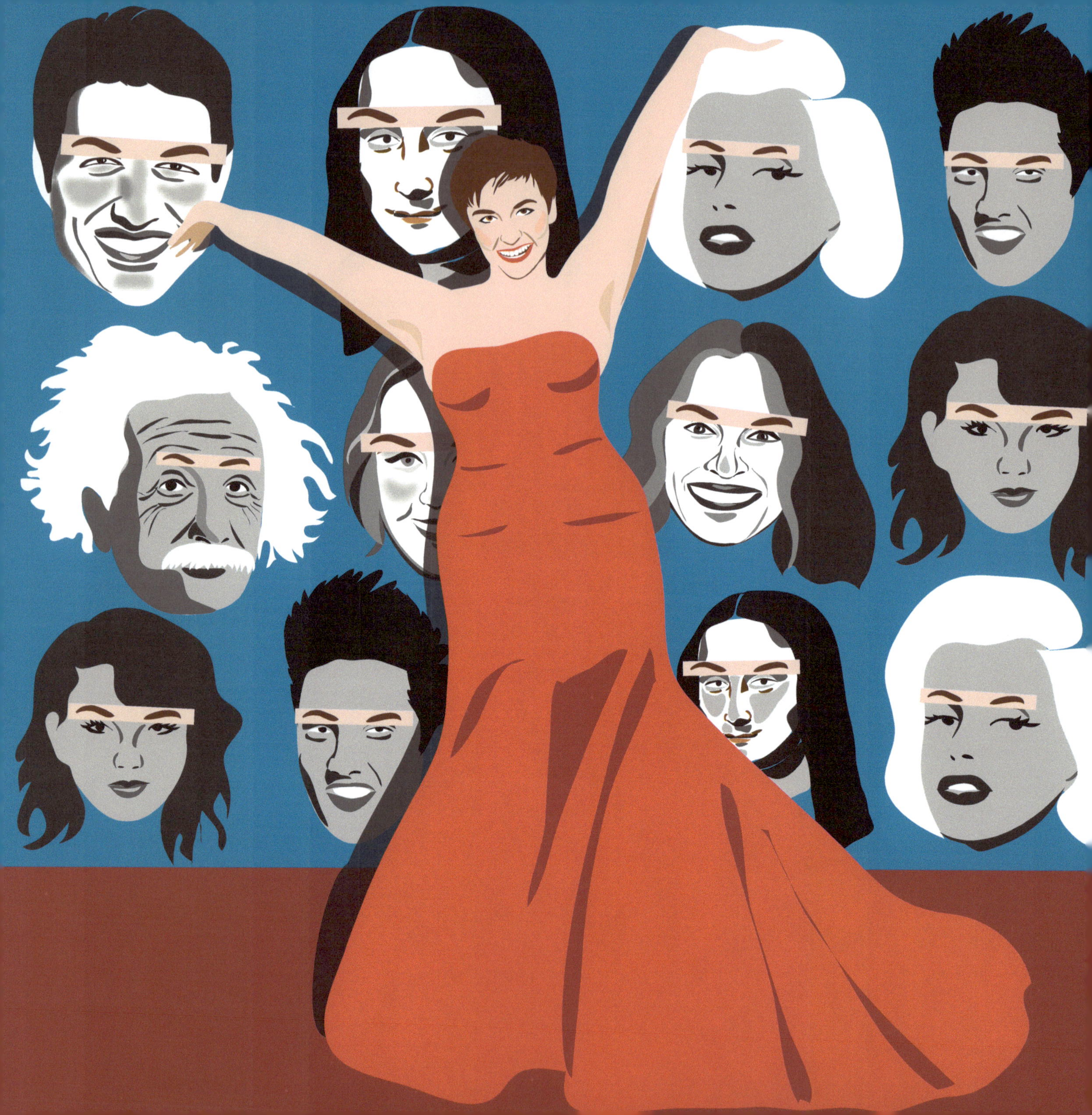

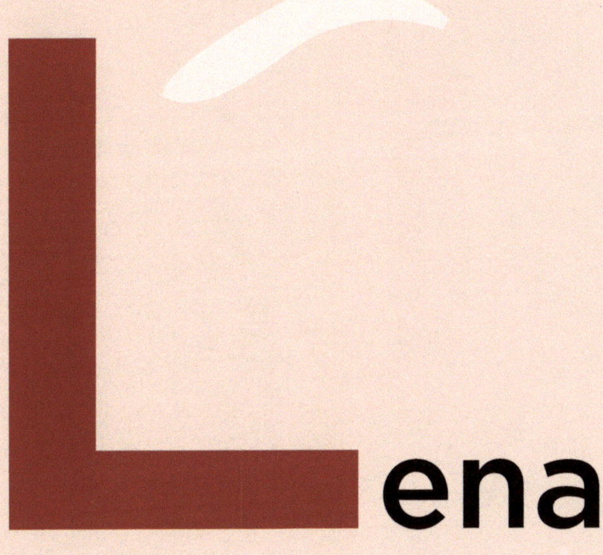

Lena

Behold! the Lena Brow!
All hail her comic genius!
Haters only hate her
'Cuz she doesn't have a man part.

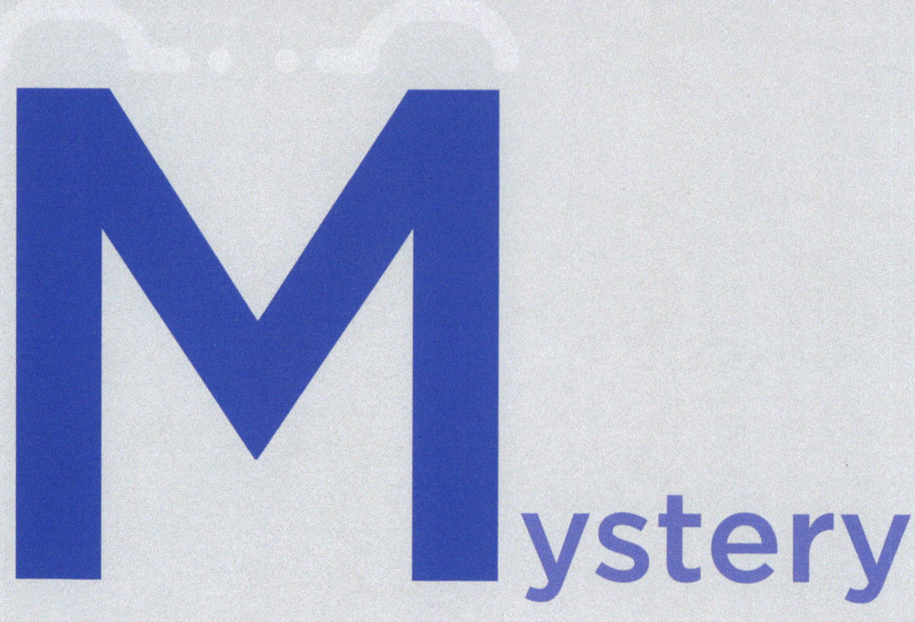

Mystery

Anna Wintour wears her hair in a
pin-straight bob
With bangs draped like an iron curtain.
Her brows are hidden behind them—why?
No one can say for certain.

What do they look like?
No one knows!
What's the answer to this mystery?
Here's what we propose:

One morning Anna looked in the mirror
and moaned
"Oh hell, I'm plumb out of luck!
These tweezers are duller than *Ladies'
Home Journal*
And my brow stubble is too short to pluck.

"I can't go to work like this.
I look totally ridiculous!"

She stared out her bathroom window
The sun was up, and she was nearly in
tears
Then the morning star's rays
Redirected her gaze
Toward a pair of gold-plated shears.

Anna grabbed the scissors
And with those shears, her hair was shorn
She cut bangs to hide
Brows she couldn't abide
And voilà! A style icon was born.

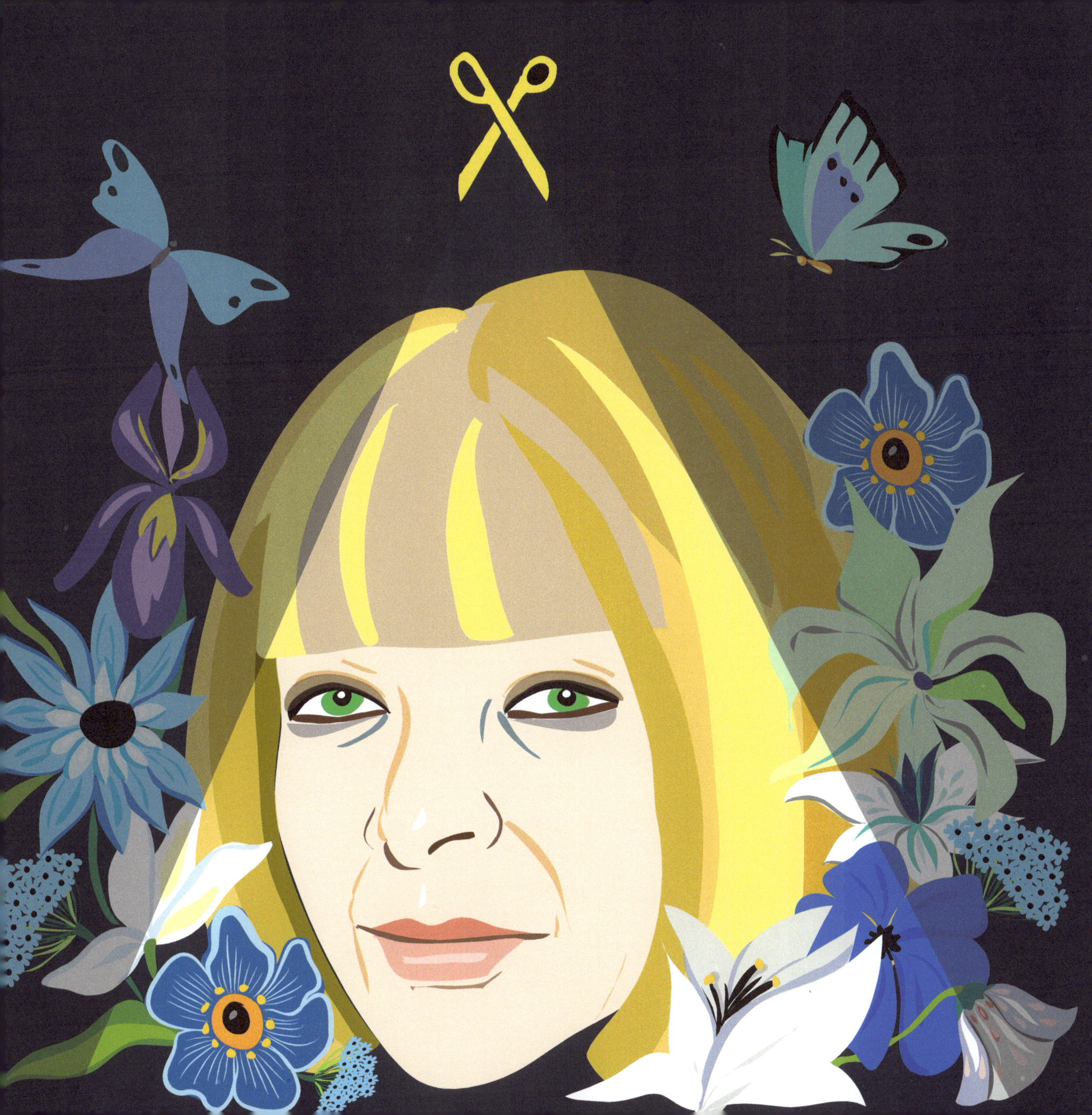

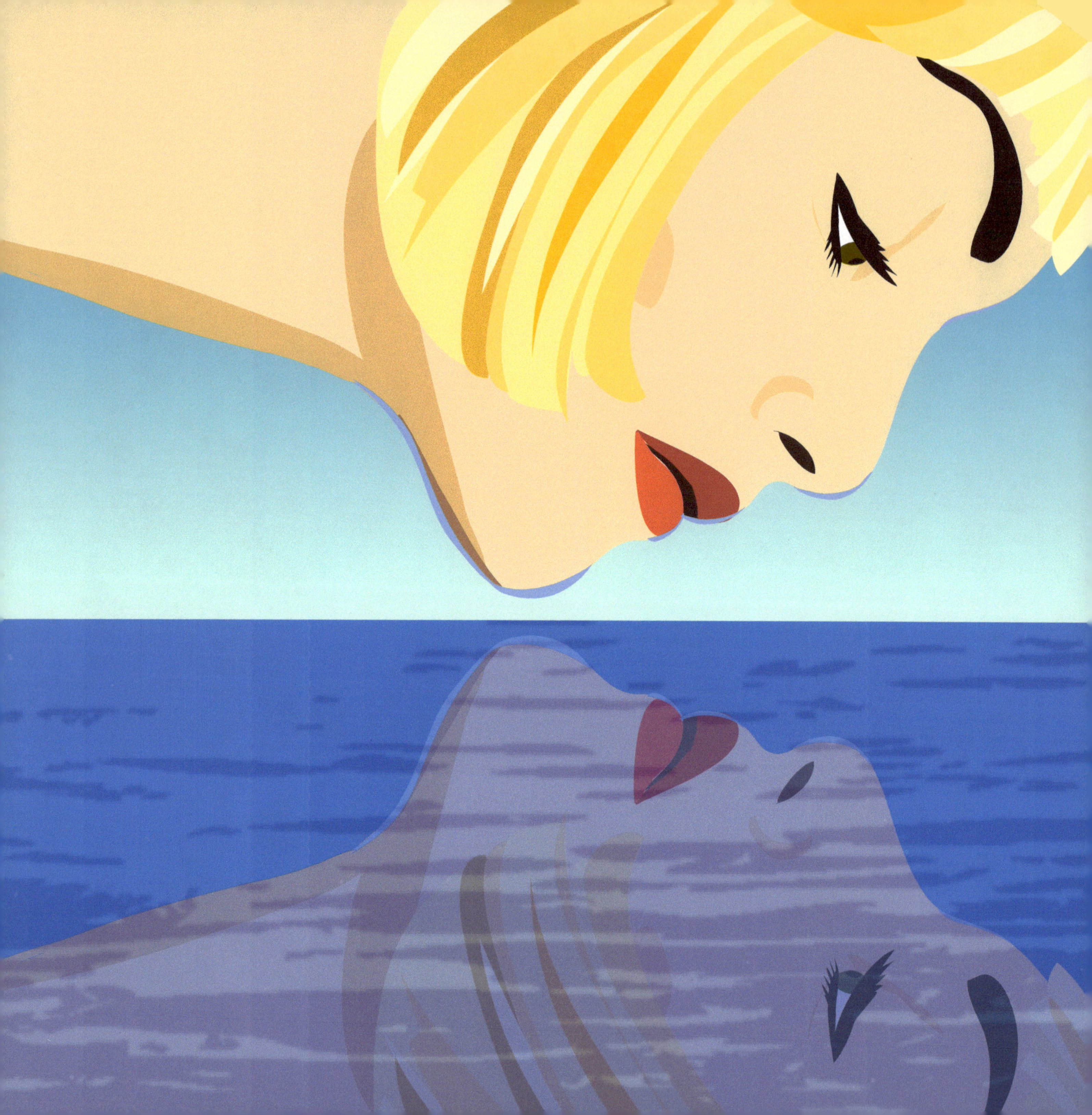

Narcissus

You know you envy Narcissus's brows;
They're as beautiful as beautiful can be
When you see them you can't take your eyes away
And frankly, neither can she.

Ocelot

Jocelyn wanted to look like a tiger
And then to look like a lion
So she made her face rather catlike
And into her business, folks started pryin'.

If only she'd given the tweezers a chance
She could have plucked the brow of an ocelot
And instead of being called Bride of Wildenstein
She'd now be known as Ms. Jocelot!

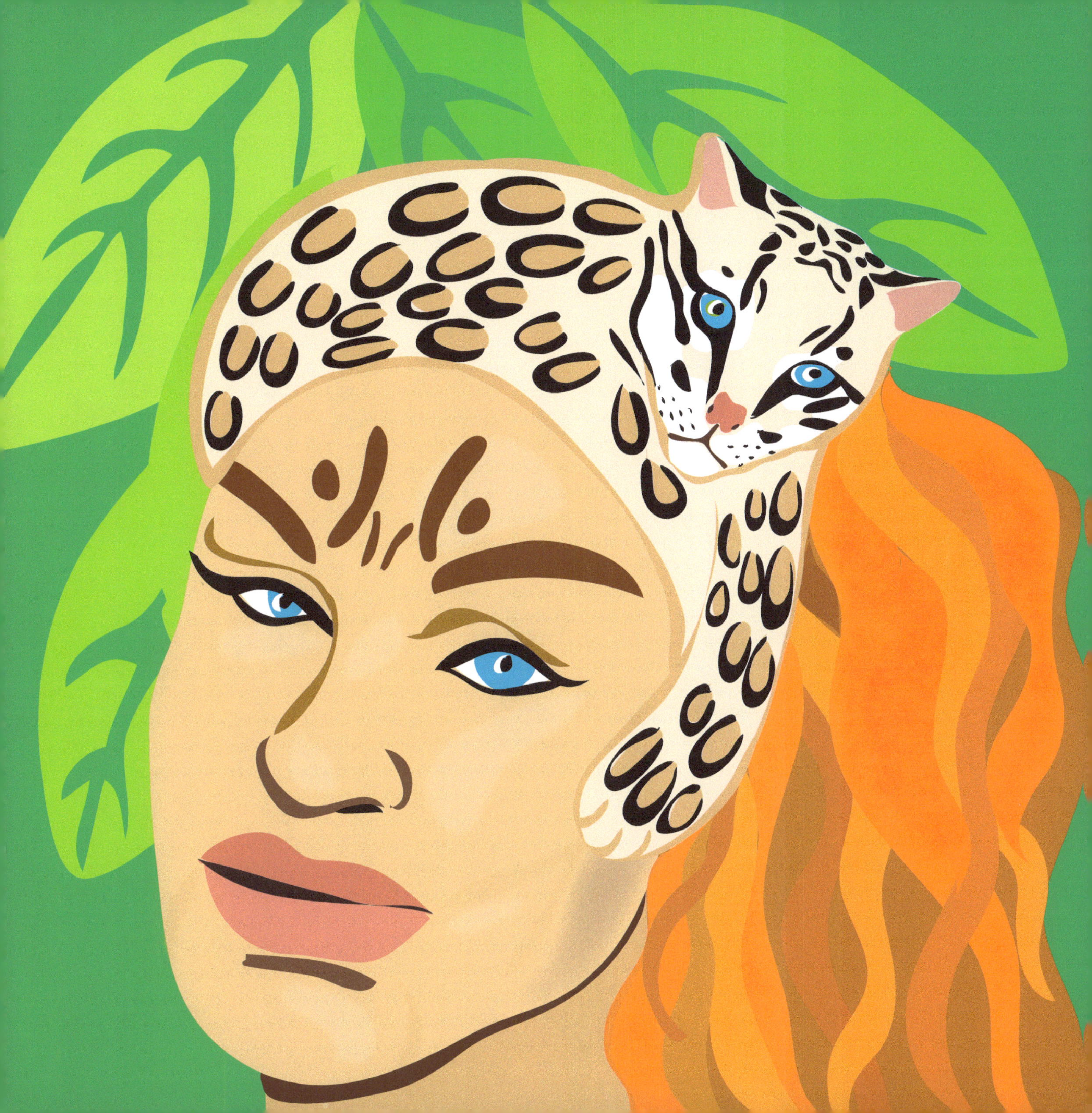

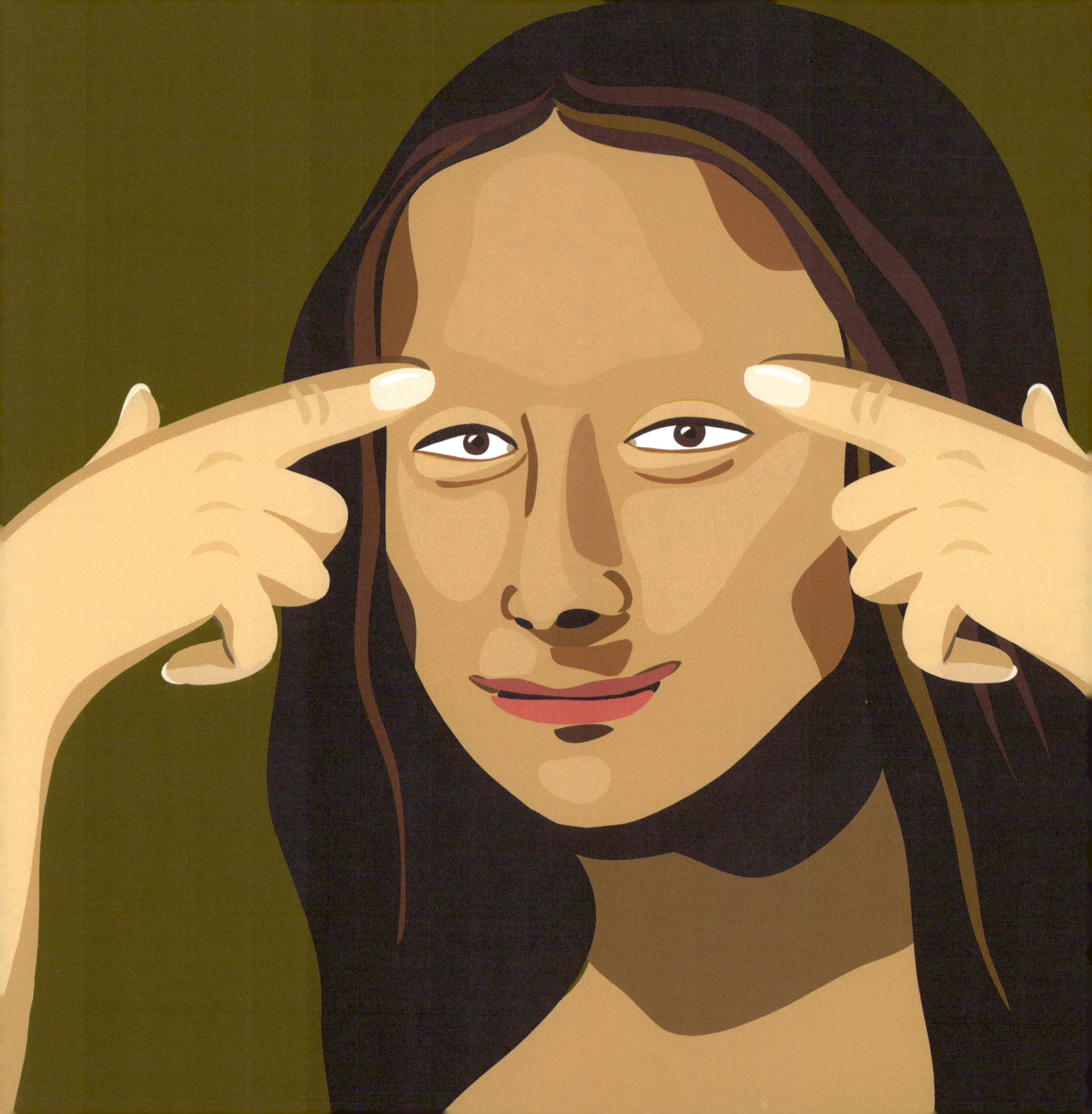

Placebo

When I first put on my 'Cebos
I was like: "Hm, these feel a bit stiff."
But then I ran my fingers across them
And could hardly tell the diff!

—Lisa

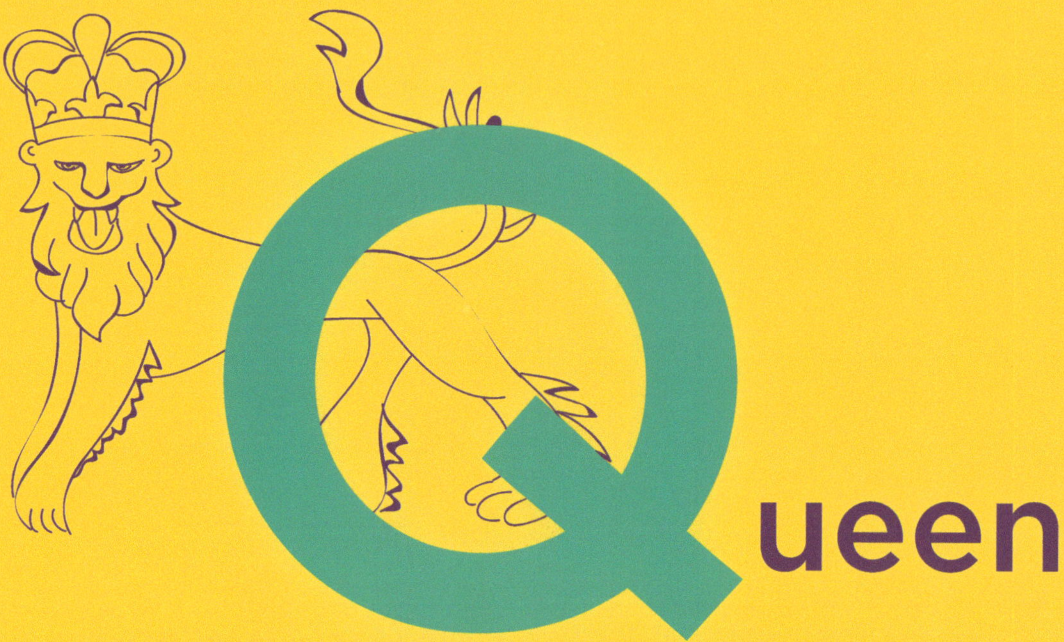

Queen

There are so many queens
Whose brows get attention
But Queen Elizabeth II's
Deserve special mention.

During the Second World War
Her country was doing battle
With the super-evil Axis powers
And her conscience this did rattle!

"All vain processions are now suspended!
Including (those stupid!) Henley Balls
It's war! Time to get down and dirty
O'Brien! Fetch my overalls!"

So Liz became a mechanic—
Fixed an engine when somebody broke it
Drove trucks while bombs fell around her
Put that in your pipe and smoke it!

Now, if you've ever dissed E's style
You've just been schooled! And to wit
You cannot deny the undeniable truth:
Queen Elizabeth's brow is the shit!

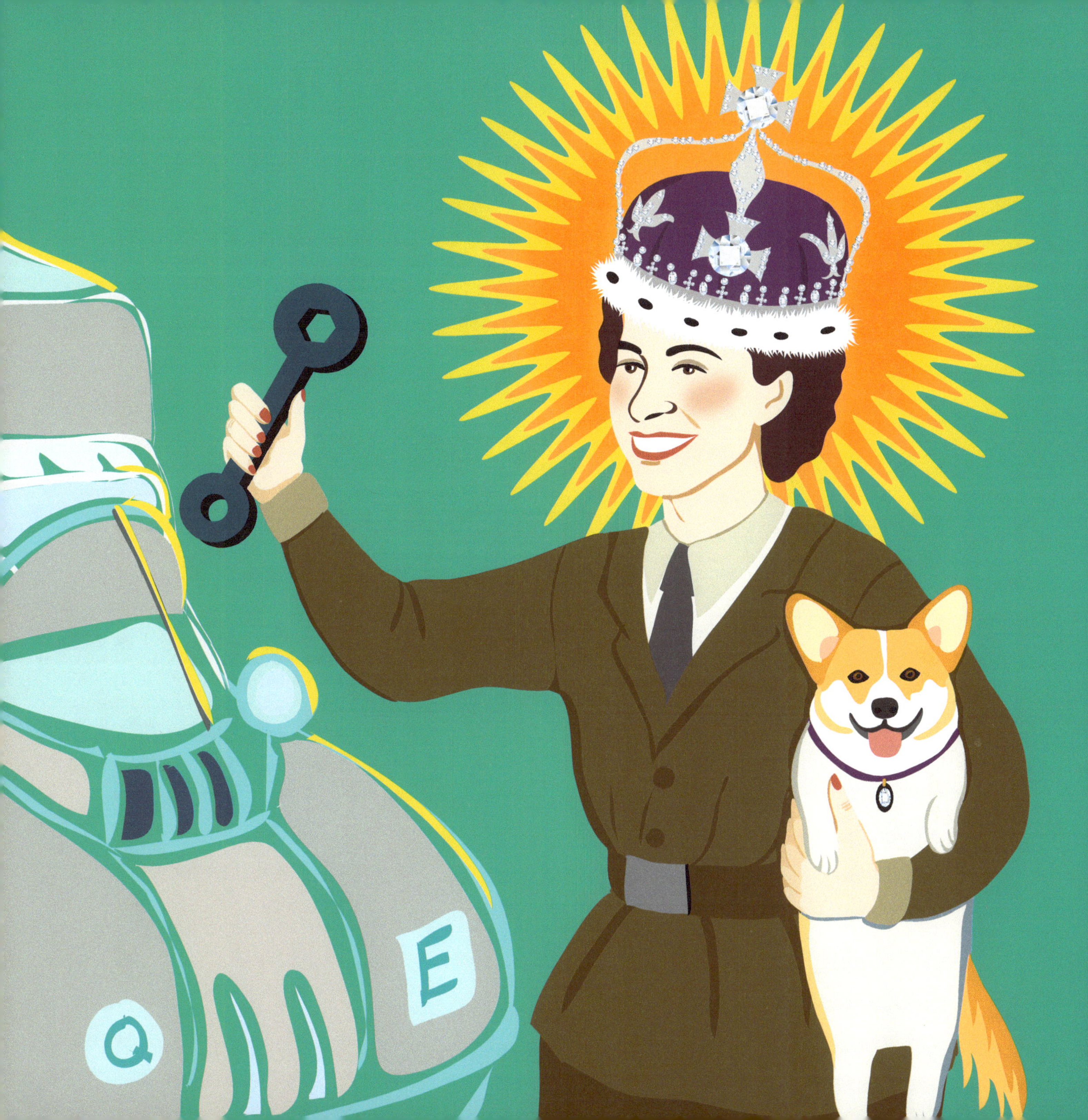
Q
E

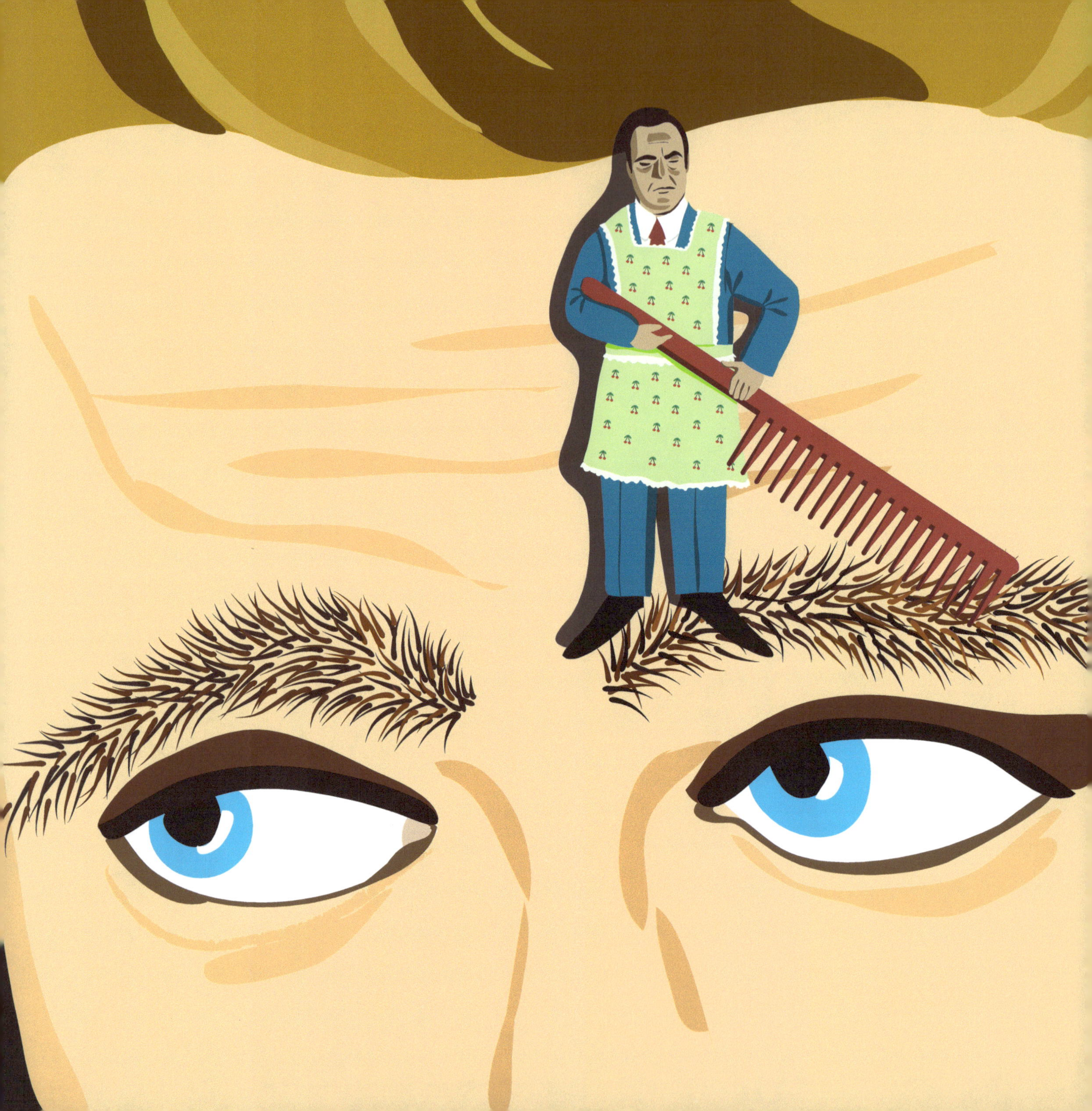

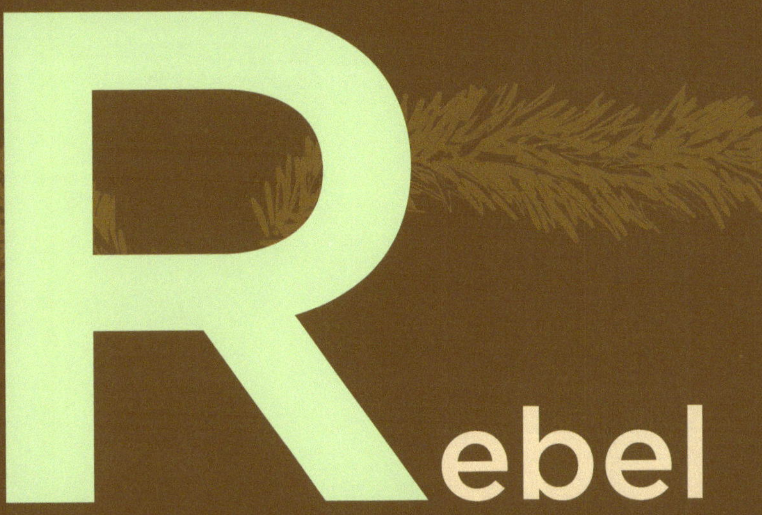

Rebel

Rebel without a Cause Brows grow in every which direction;

Their youthful indignation is no cause for vituperation.

They're only looking for a father figure, lover, or best friend to say,

"Don't sweat the existential angst, it will all turn out OK!"

Sisyphus

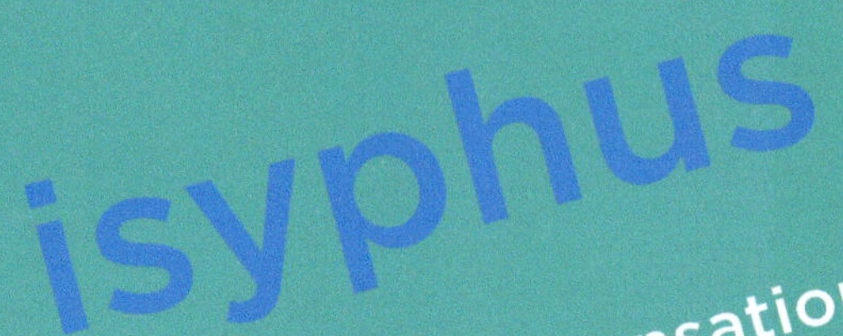

The Sisyphus Brow is a nagging sensation:
You pluck week after week
Then end up assuming
That eyebrow grooming
Is absurdity at its peak

But take heart intrepid plucker
Whether you believe in fate or volition
There are millions like you
From Oprah to Camus
Who pluck on despite the human condition.

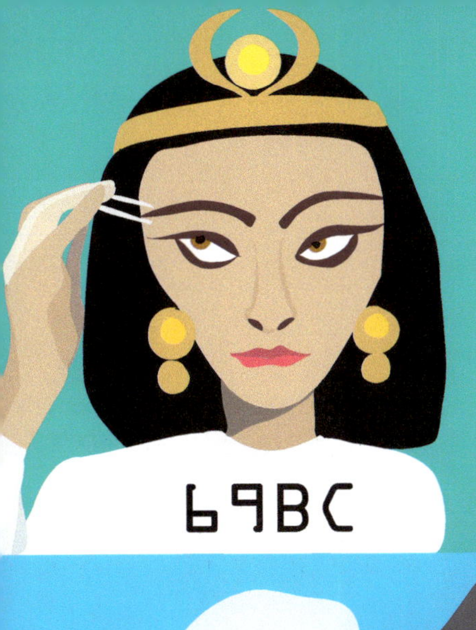
69BC
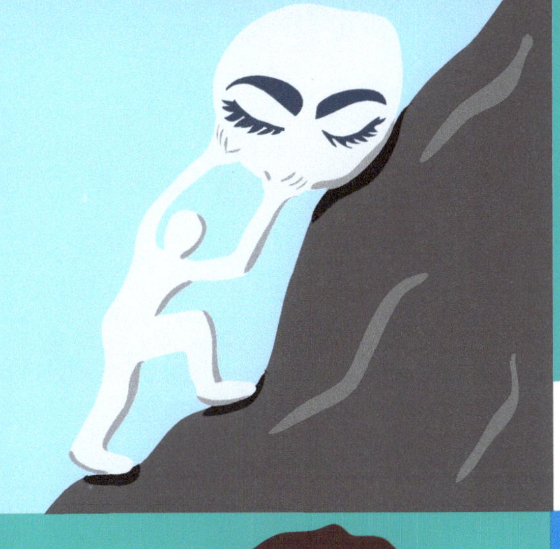
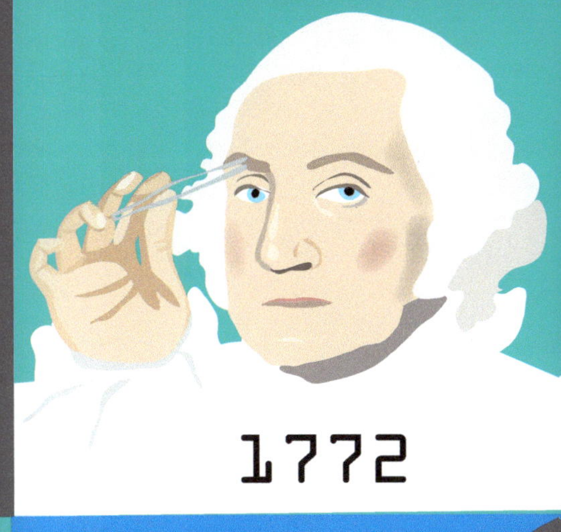
1772
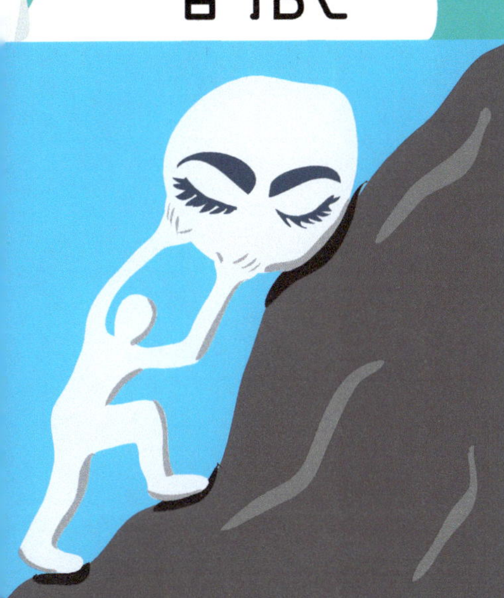
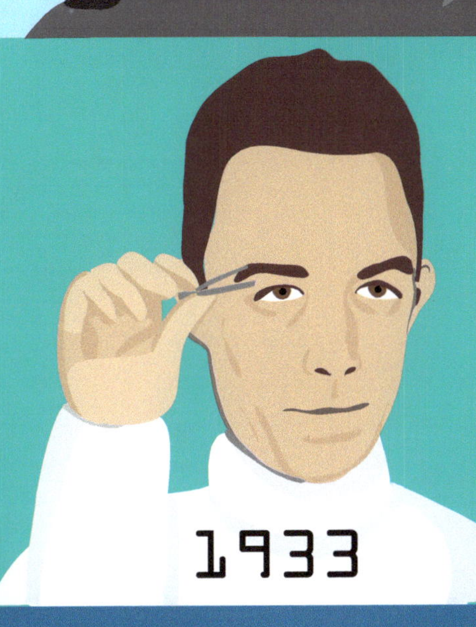
1933
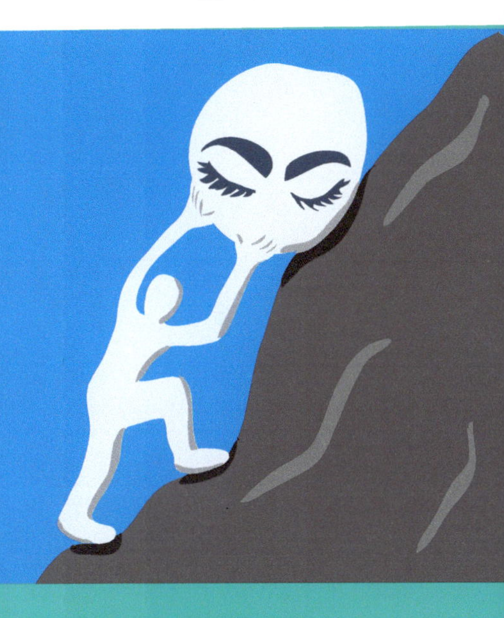
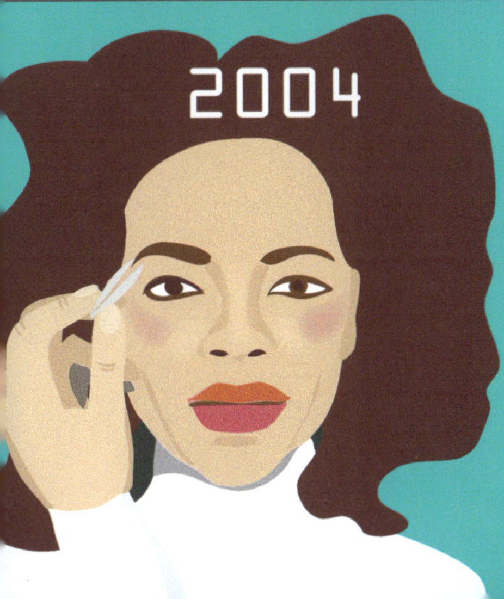
2004
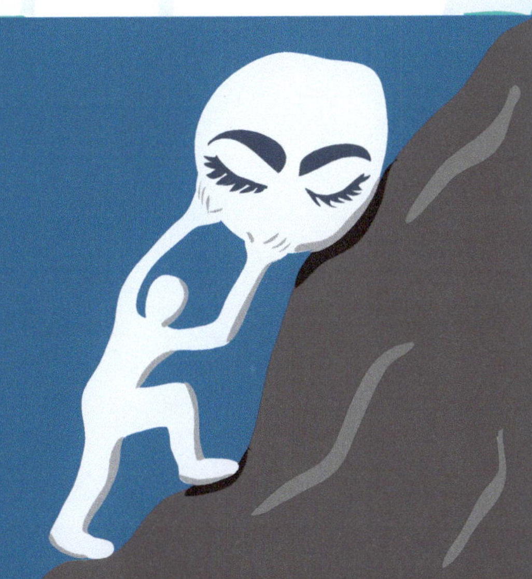
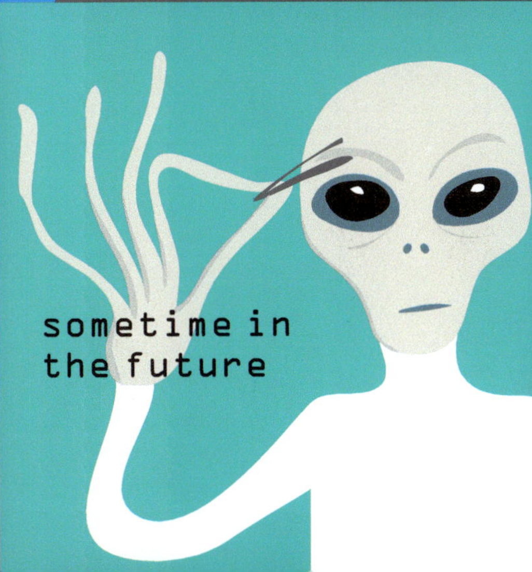
sometime in
the future

Transcendental

Brows ascend. Floating!
Sayonara, ol' tweezers!
Good-bye and pluck you.

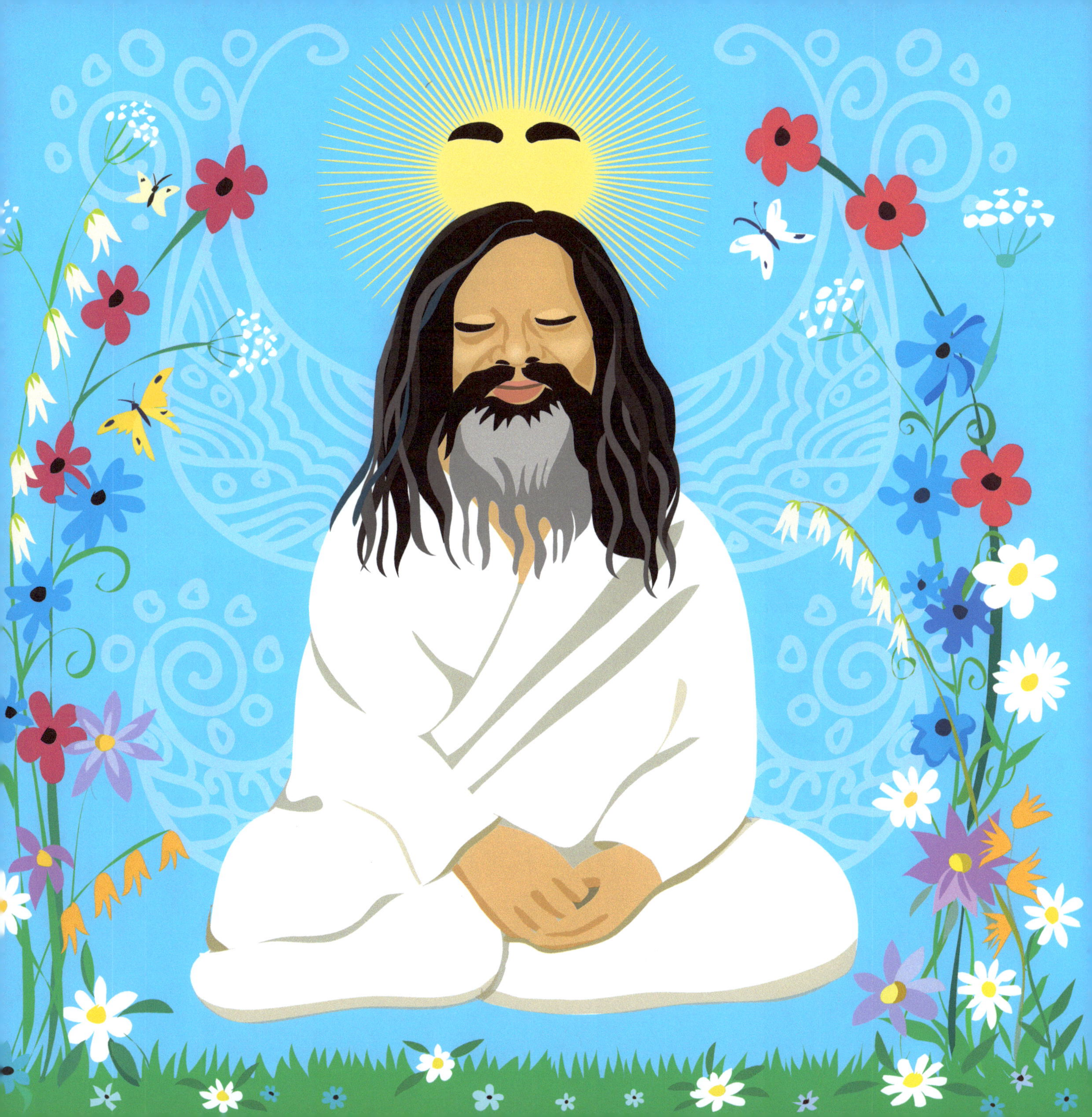

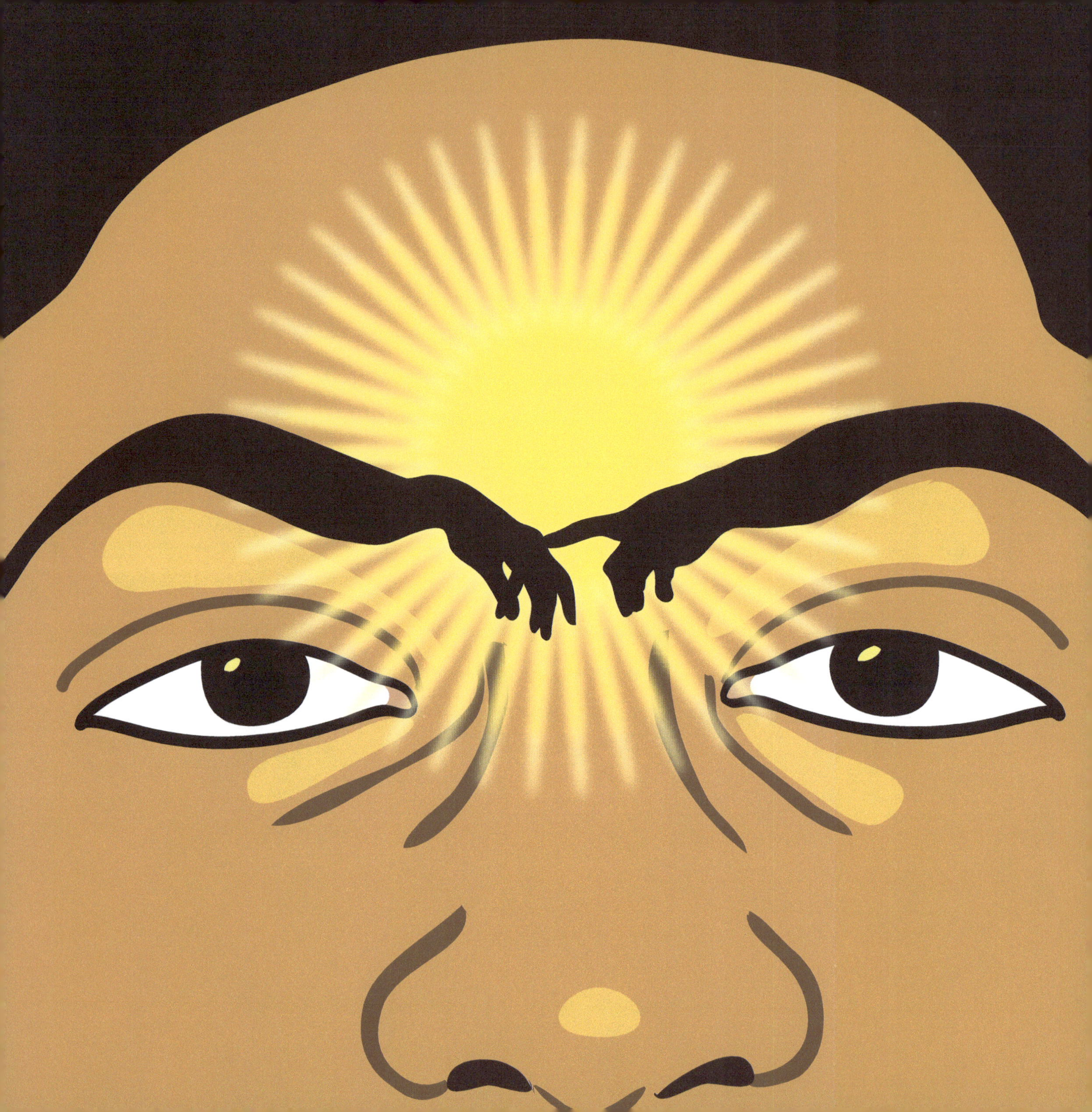

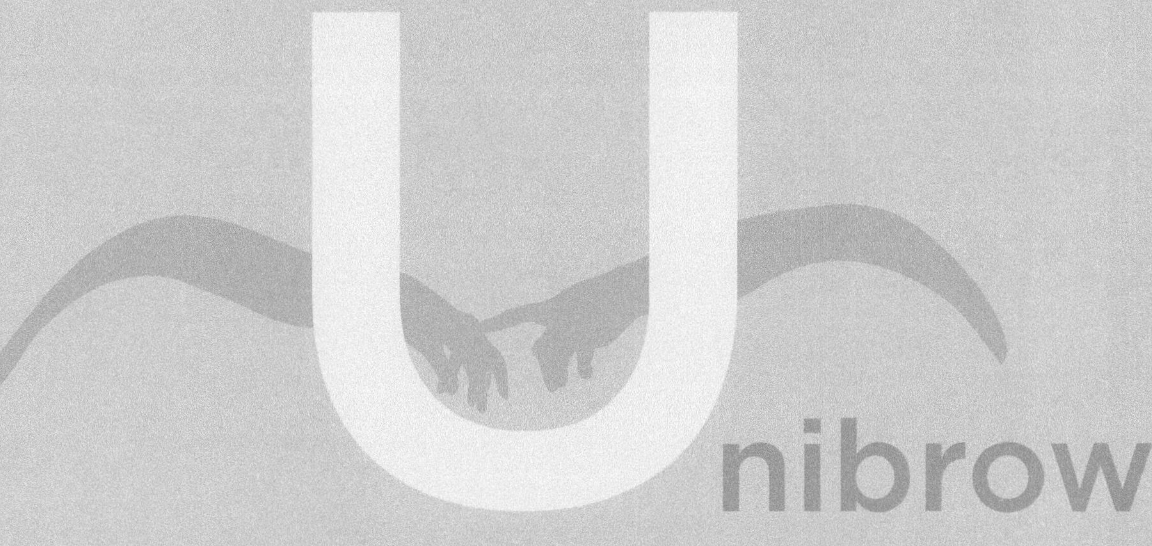

Unibrow

Some eyebrows yearn to unite
So why do we keep them apart?
Plucking the space between them
Just breaks their poor little hearts.

So save the tweezers for splinters
Don't be a plucking son-of-a-mother
Don't lay on the hurt
Be like *Sesame Street*'s Bert:
Let each brow connect with his brother.

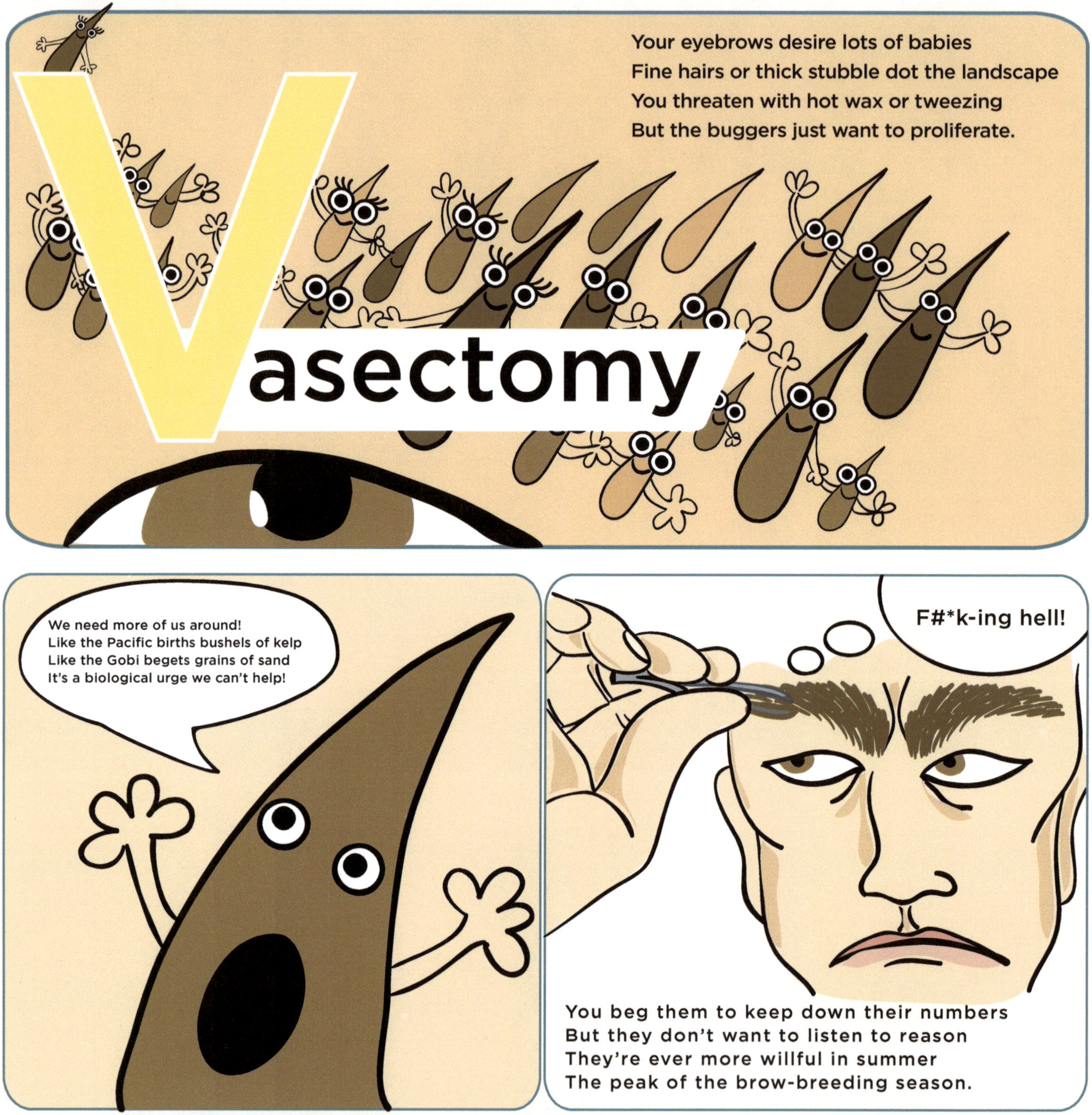

Vasectomy

Your eyebrows desire lots of babies
Fine hairs or thick stubble dot the landscape
You threaten with hot wax or tweezing
But the buggers just want to proliferate.

You beg them to keep down their numbers
But they don't want to listen to reason
They're ever more willful in summer
The peak of the brow-breeding season.

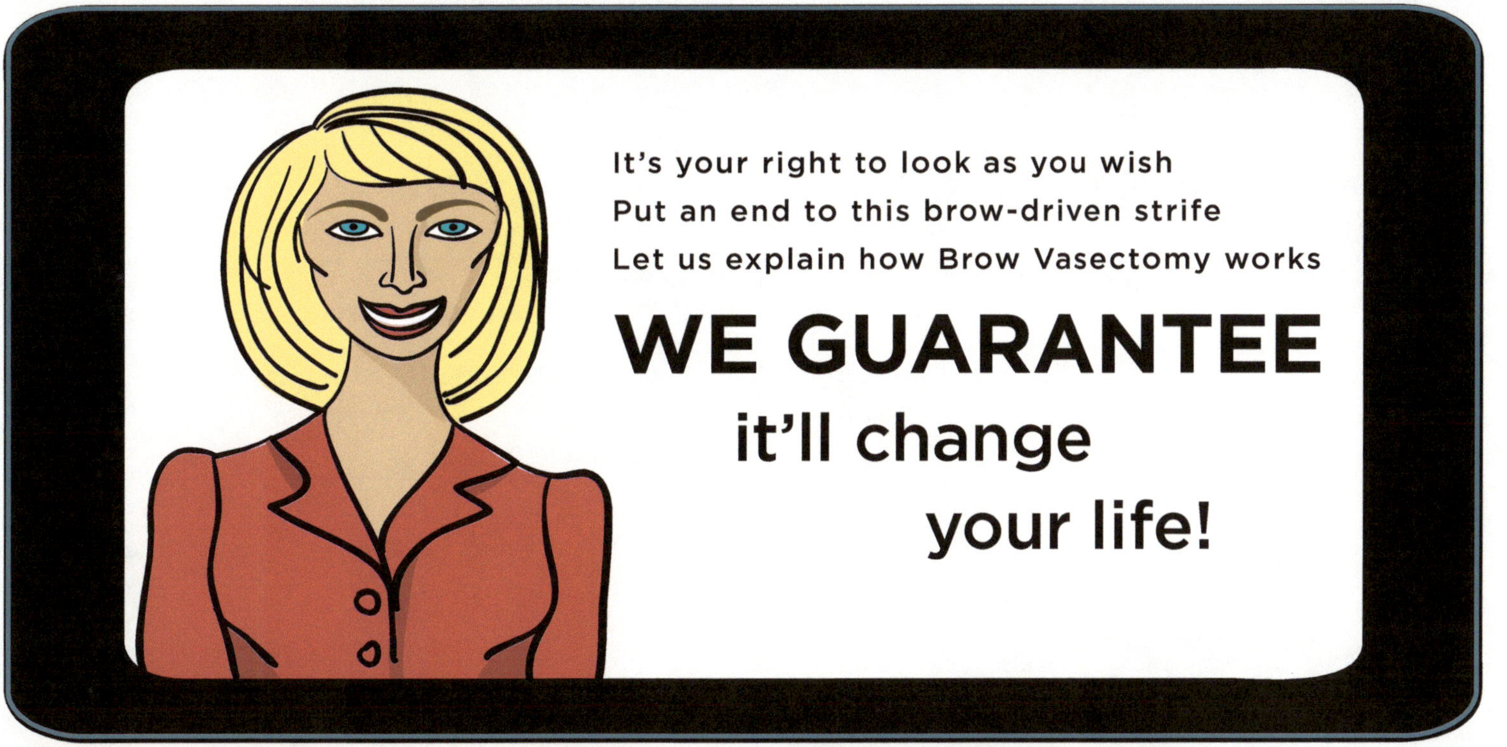

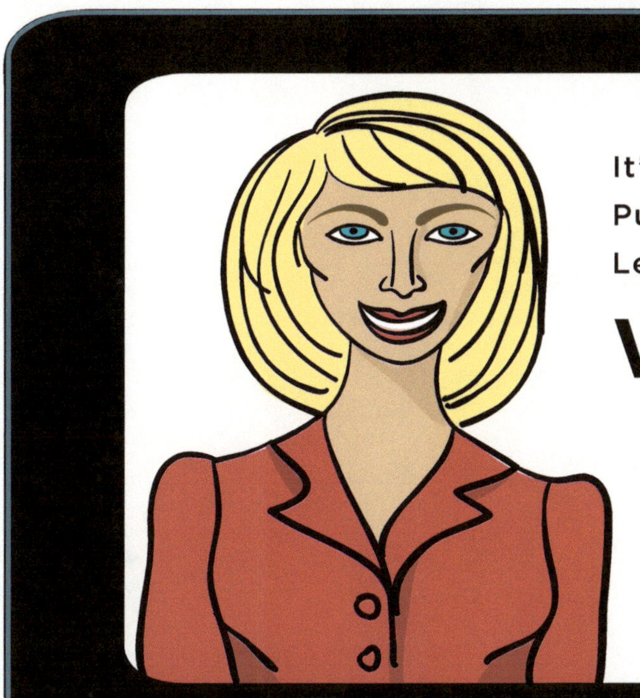

It's your right to look as you wish
Put an end to this brow-driven strife
Let us explain how Brow Vasectomy works

WE GUARANTEE
it'll change
your life!

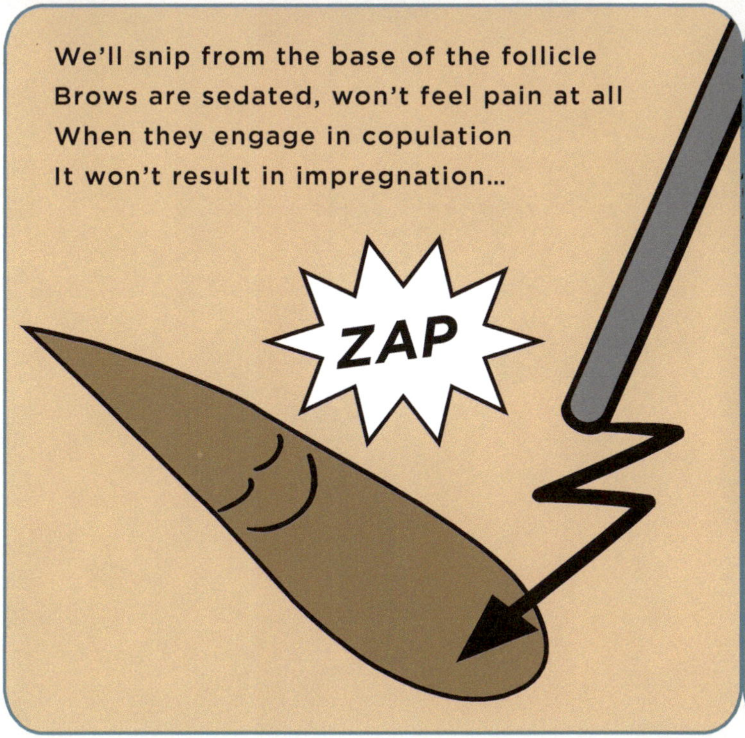

We'll snip from the base of the follicle
Brows are sedated, won't feel pain at all
When they engage in copulation
It won't result in impregnation...

ZAP

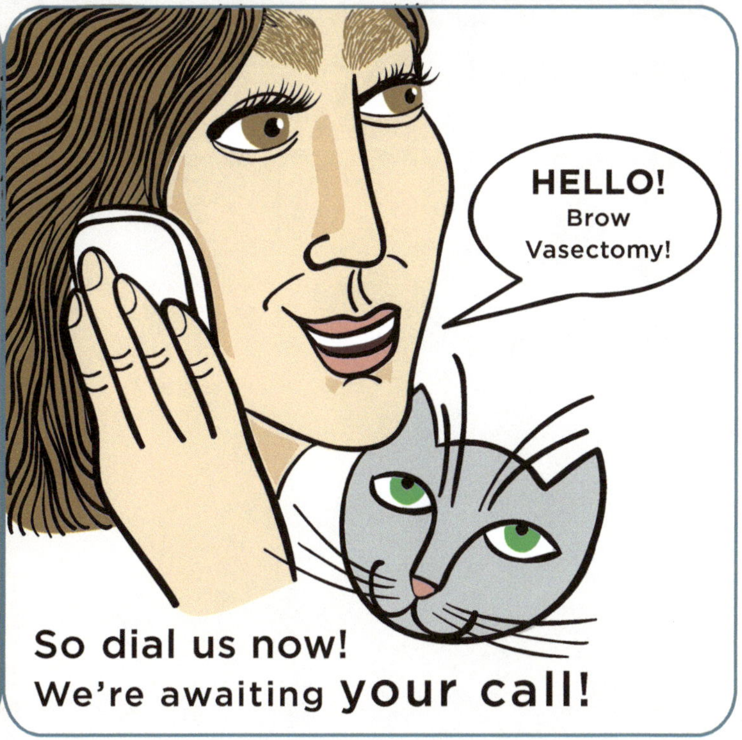

HELLO!
Brow
Vasectomy!

So dial us now!
We're awaiting **your call!**

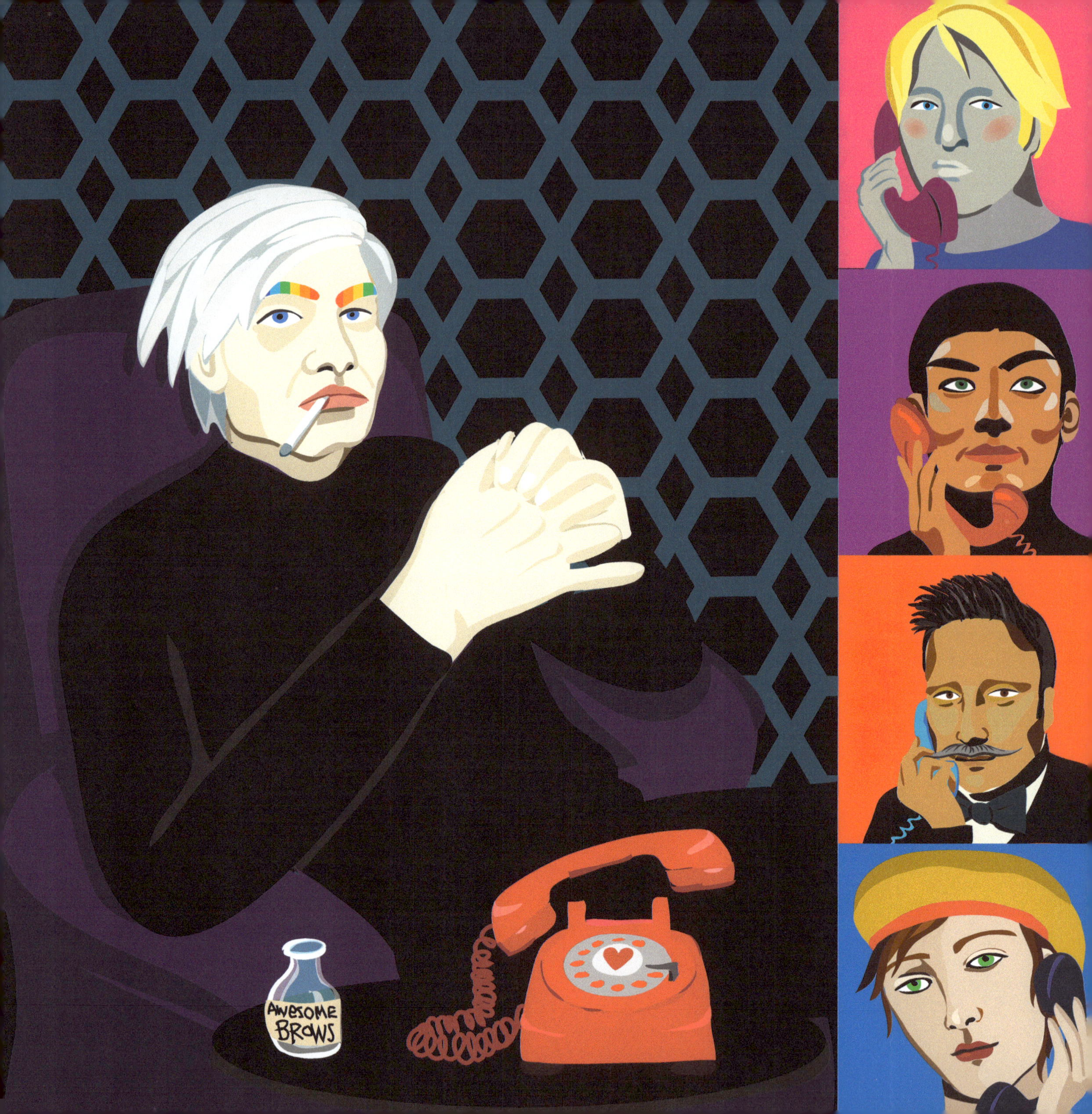
AWESOME
BROWS

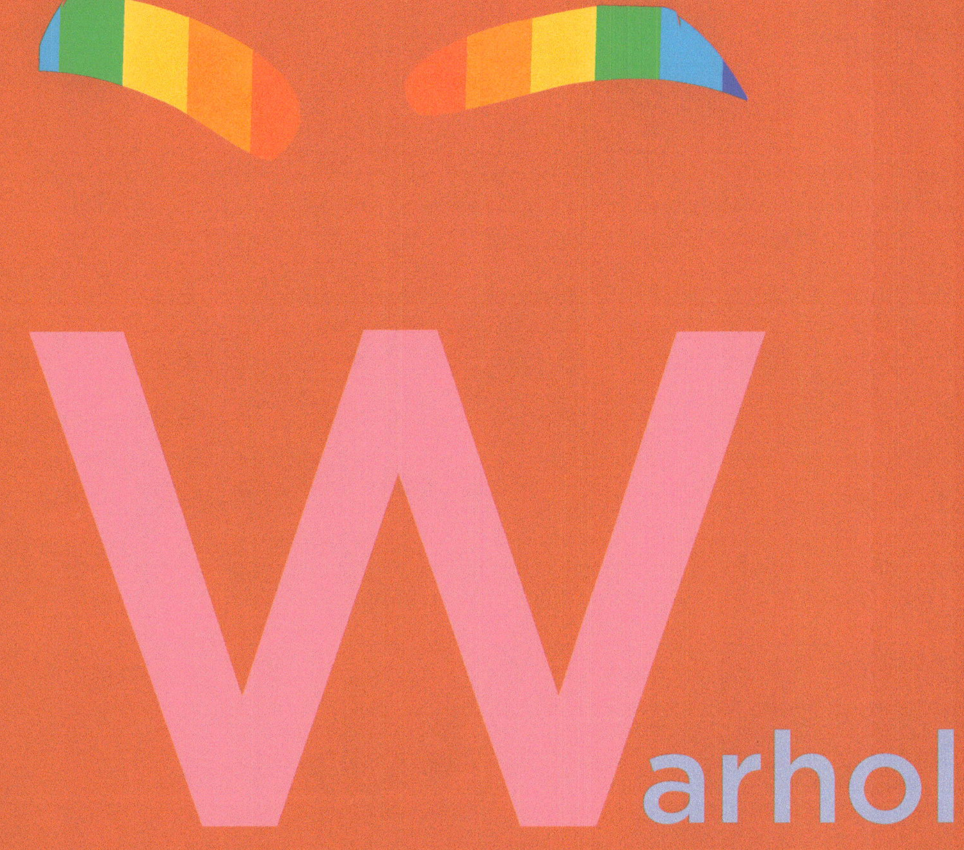

Warhol

My Campbell soup cans generate tons of *Wows*!
Fans flock to me like carnivores to cows.
Though I get lots of dates
With super-hot potential mates,
I'd rather stay home and dye my brows.

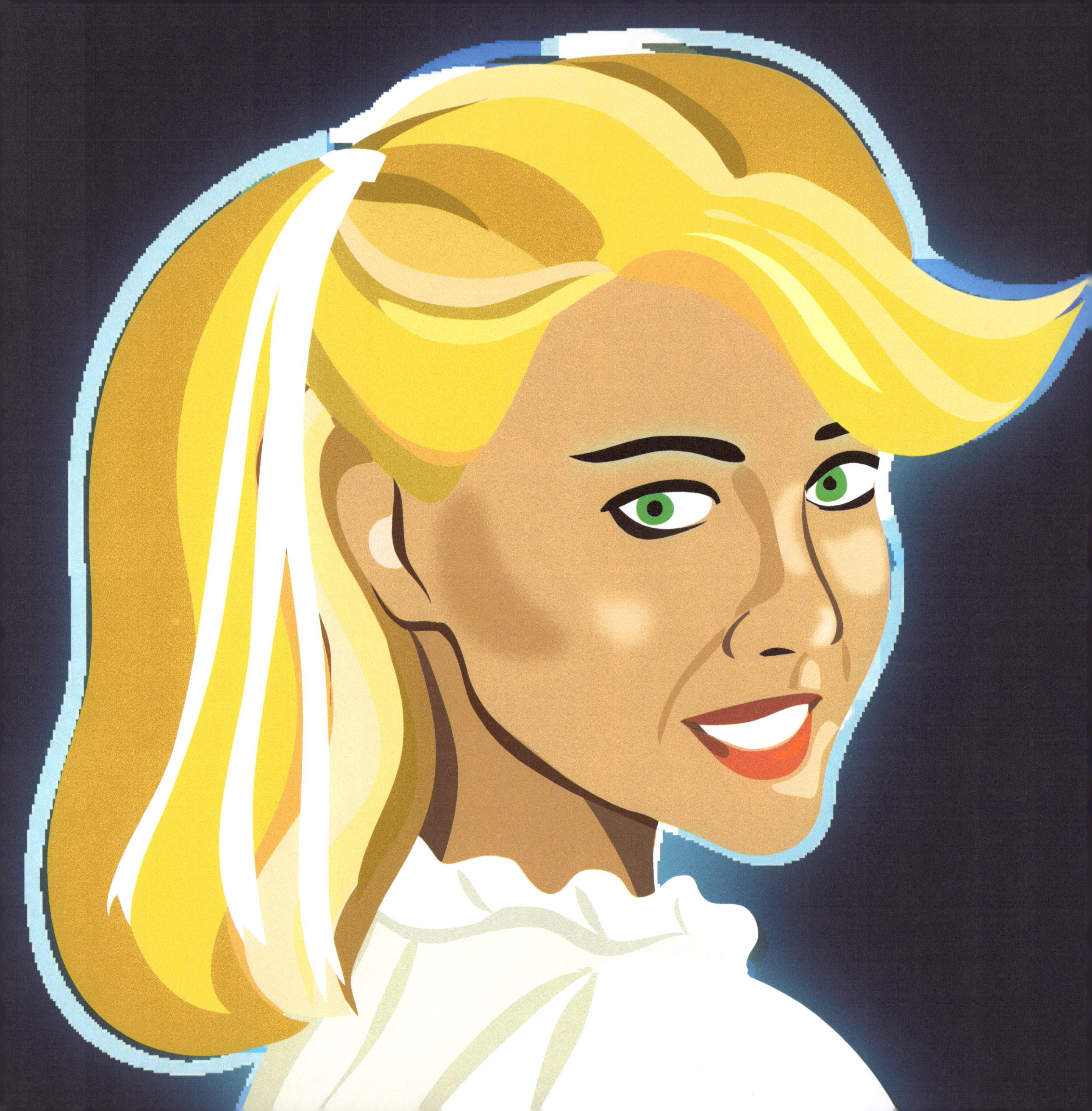

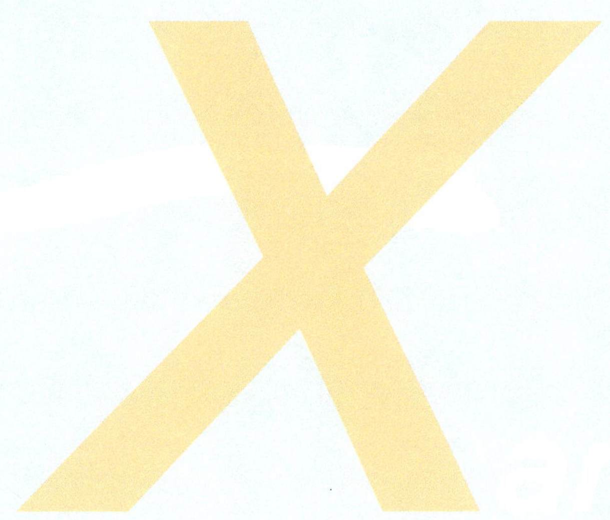

Remember the ’80s film *Xanadu*?
Critics collectively screamed, “Let’s pan it!”
But a few of us in our heart of hearts whispered:
“This movie’s awesome and I love it, goddamn it!”

It’s kinda the same with eyebrows!
One’s disaster is another one’s prize
Truth is few of us know what we’re doing—
One can only succeed if one tries.

So ignore those who trash-talk your brow
True fans will proclaim: “I want it!”
Like Olivia skating through space
Blonde waves locked in a hair spray’s embrace
Xanadu Brow: Get out there and flaunt it!

Yakuza

Yakuza Brows are elaborate tattoos
Beautifully rendered and never dinky
And if you should dare to insult them
You'll have to cut off your pinky.

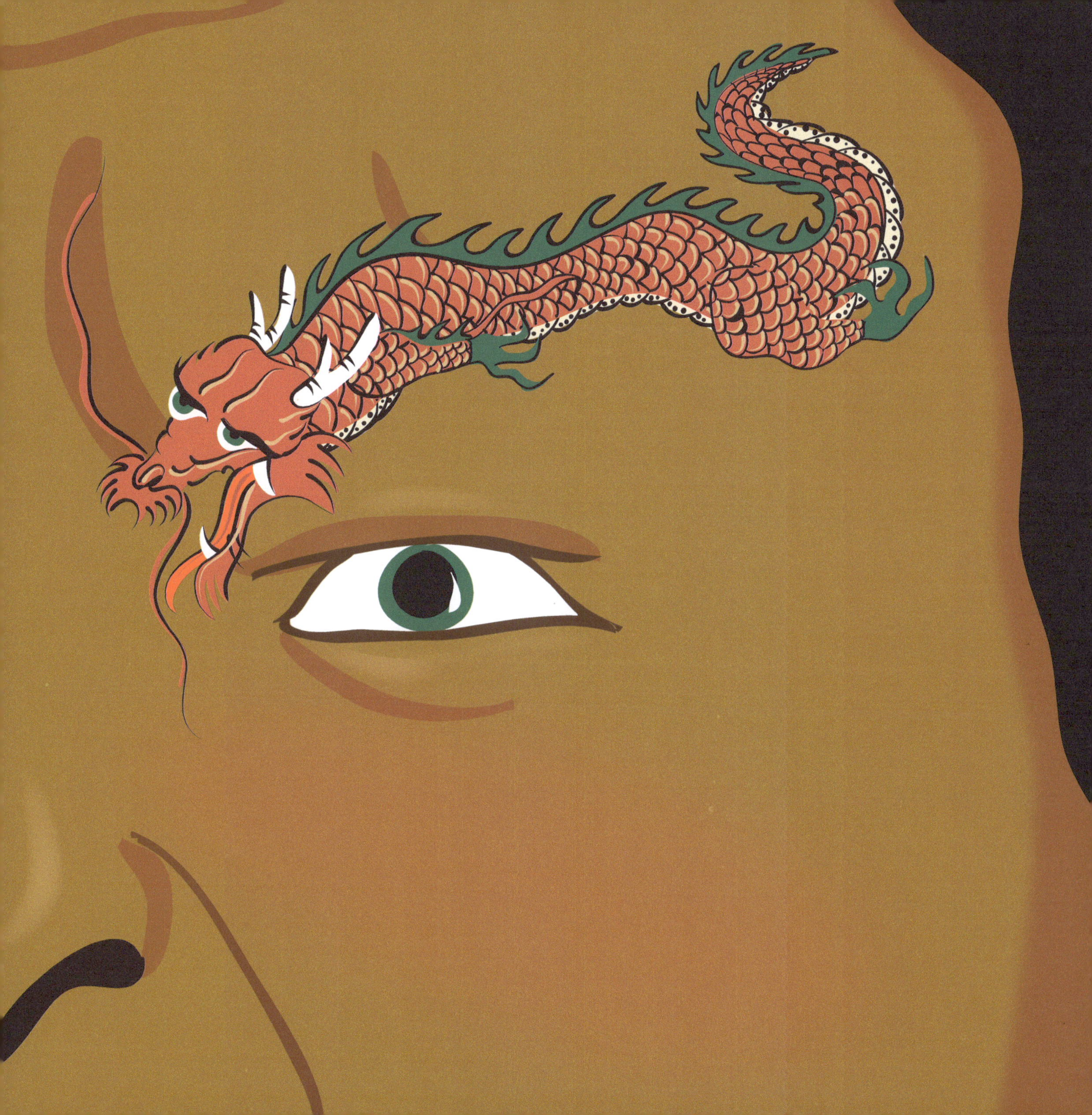

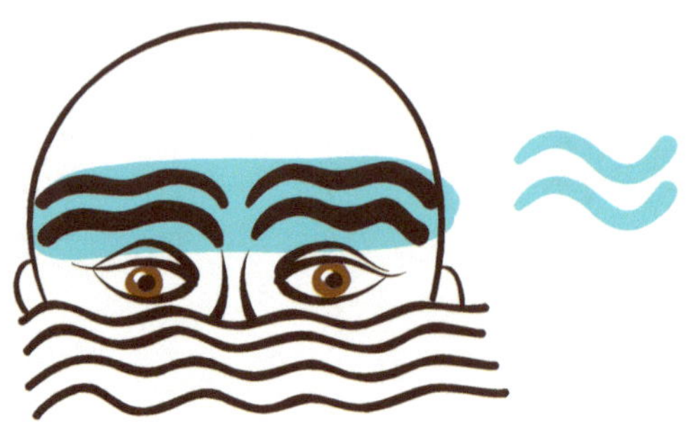

Aquarius: The Water Bearer

JANUARY 21–FEBRUARY 20

Your brows want to heal the world
Feed the poor, teach kids in the 'hood
It's OK you're not Jesus,
Grab your brow-brush and tweeze-us
And pluck for the greater good.

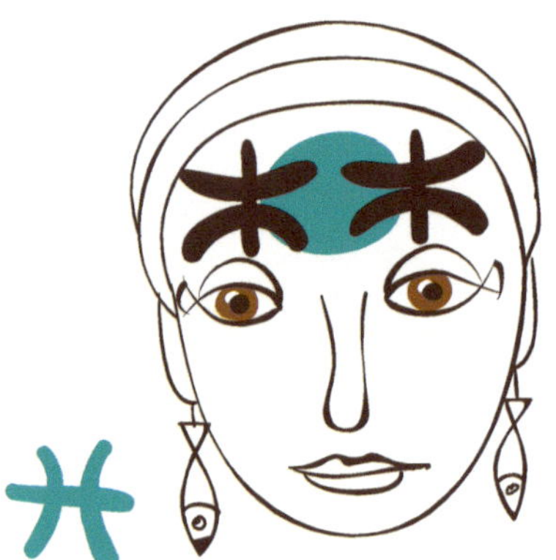

Pisces: The Fishes

FEBRUARY 21–MARCH 20

Give your arches time to rebound
For in love, fish brows can be stupid
They hate to be alone
And to depression they are prone—
Especially when plucked over by Cupid

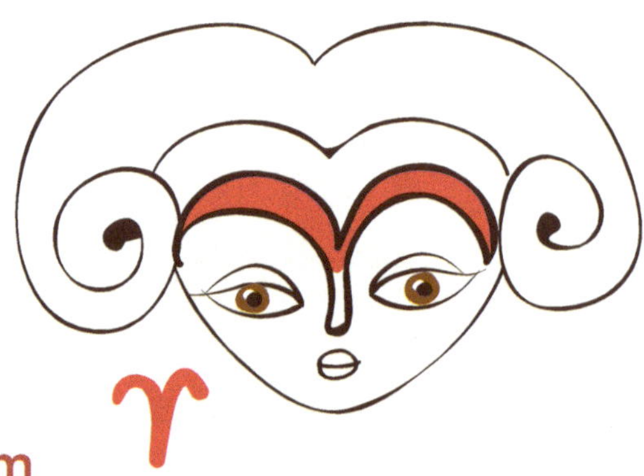

Aries: The Ram

MARCH 21–APRIL 20

You've got wild and woolly brows,
To their adventurous spirits do cater
A rollicking trip to the moon
Would make their little hearts swoon
So pluck now and worry later.

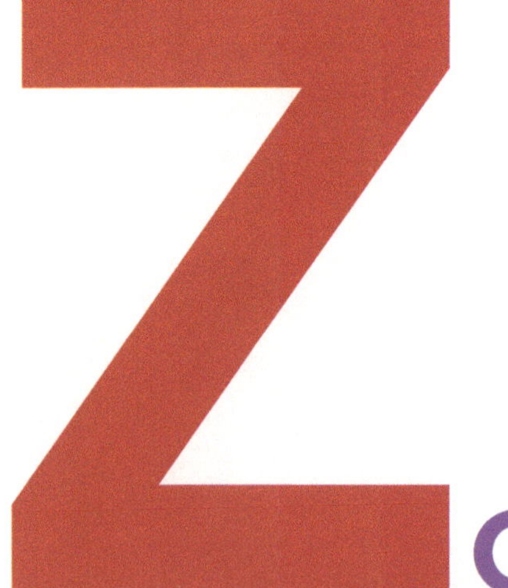

Zodiac

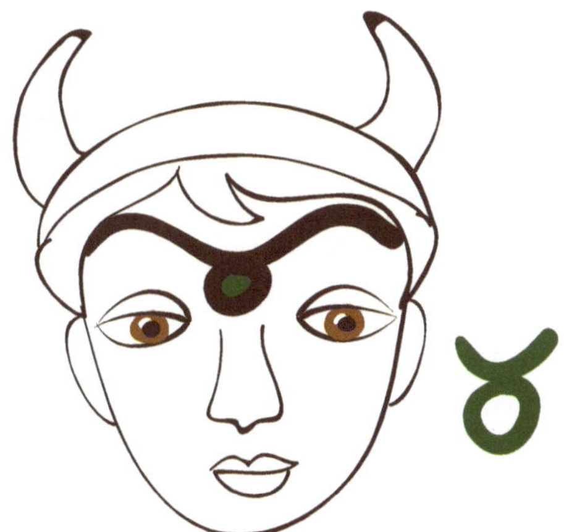

Taurus: The Bull

APRIL 21–MAY 20

With brows stubborn to the core
They stand apart from all the rest
Their "baggage" is bulky
Which is why they act sulky
So plucking them gently is best.

Gemini: The Twins

MAY 21–JUNE 20

You possess twin "It-Brows"
Who incite envy AND felicity
So when folks get jealous
Let the plucking be zealous:
There's no such thing as bad publicity!

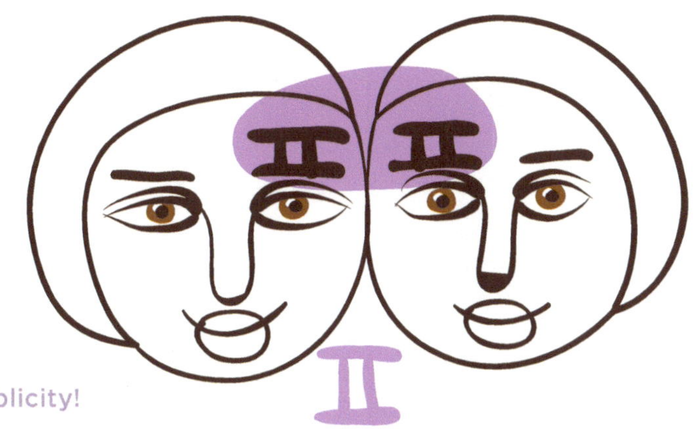

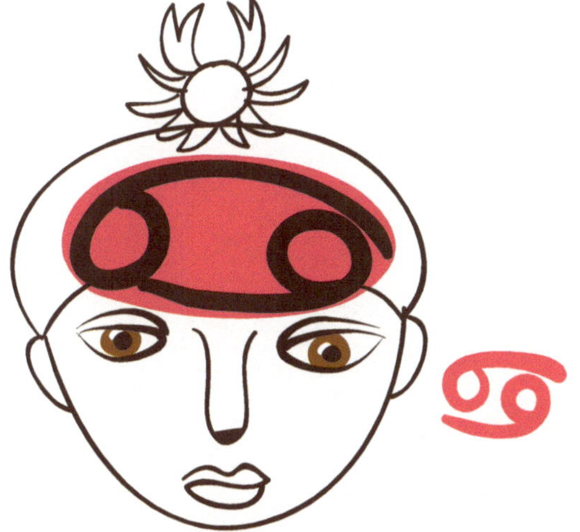

Cancer: The Crab

JUNE 21–JULY22

Cancer, you're "the Crab," and, well, crabby!
Your brows are moody but also beguiling
Sensitive and sometimes quite touchy
So pluck carefully to avoid over-riling.

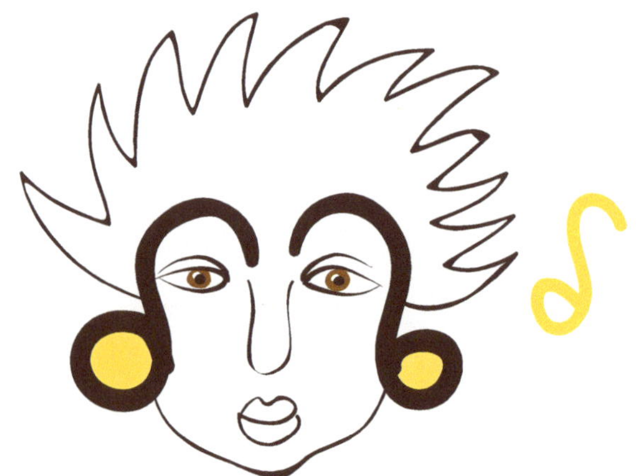

Leo: The Lion

JULY 23–AUGUST 22

Hear your arches roar!
They are faithful to the end
But if you over-pluck them
You'll never see them again.

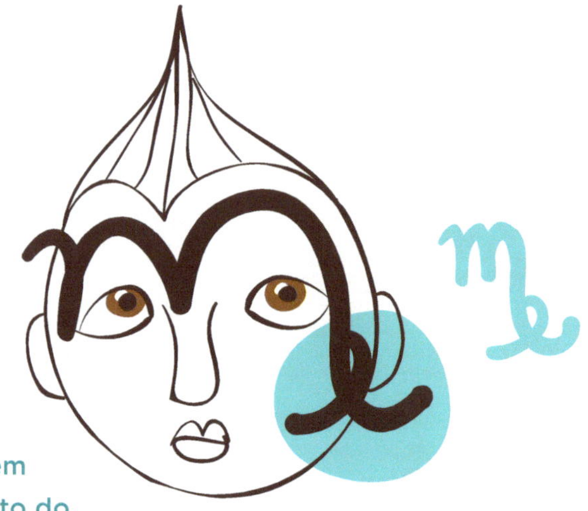

Virgo: The Virgin

AUGUST 23–SEPTEMBER 22

Your eyebrows give you their all
They're total doormats, it's true
But please don't pluck around on them
Though their kindness makes it easy to do.

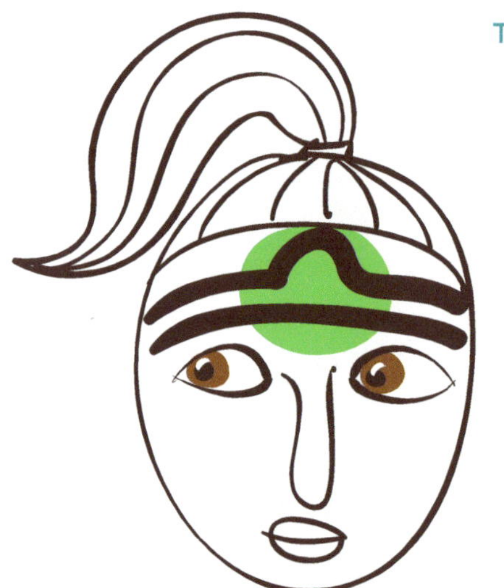

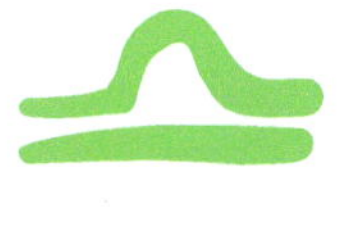

Libra: The Scales

SEPTEMBER 23–OCTOBER 22

Your brows compromise themselves
That's why they always get hurt
Don't let them get sucked up
In relationships so plucked-up
With brow-friends who treat them like dirt.

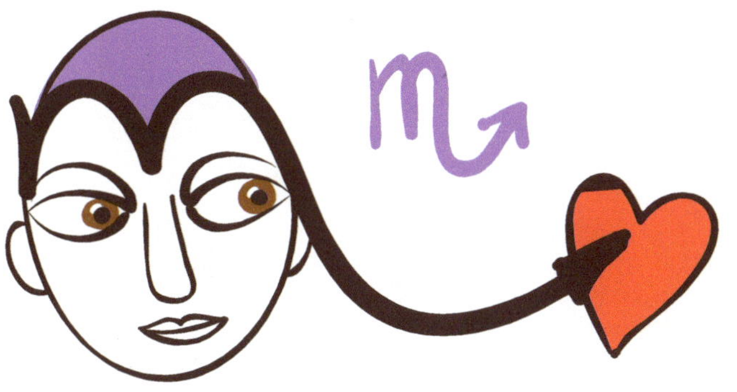

Scorpio: The Scorpion

OCTOBER 23–NOVEMBER 22

You possess the Zodiac's power-brows
Beware: Their grudges do linger
Don't even think about plucking them over
For in you they will insert their stinger.

Sagittarius: The Archer

NOVEMBER 23–DECEMBER 21

Your arches remain optimistic
Even when the future looks sucky
You may see them pout
During moments of doubt
But mostly Sag brows are quite plucky!

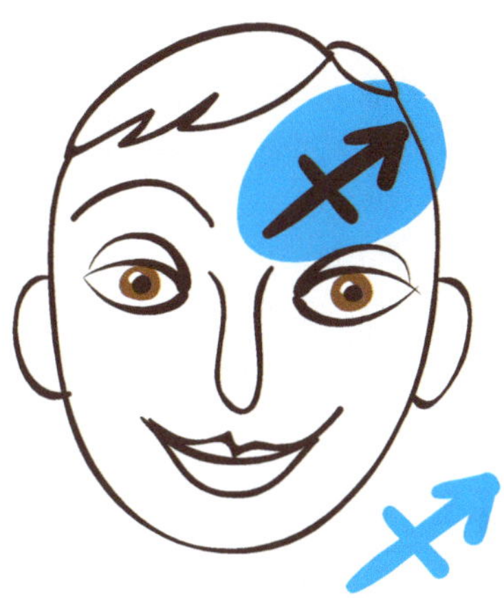

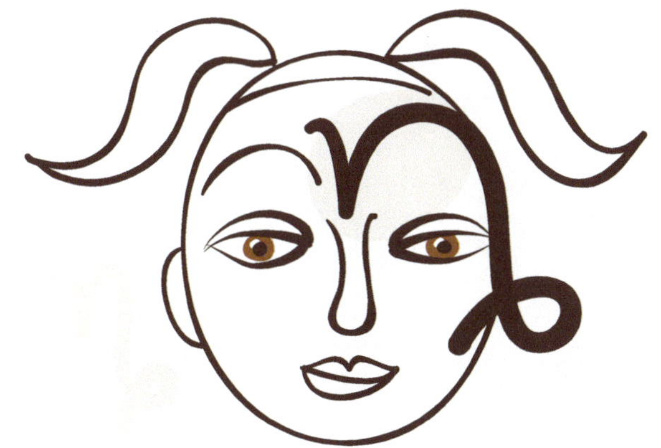

Capricorn: The Goat

DECEMBER 22–JANUARY 20

Your brows are workaholics, Cap!
They'll drive you to tweeze night and day
They want to look perfectly groomed at all costs
And won't stop 'til they get their way.

ABOUT THE AUTHORS

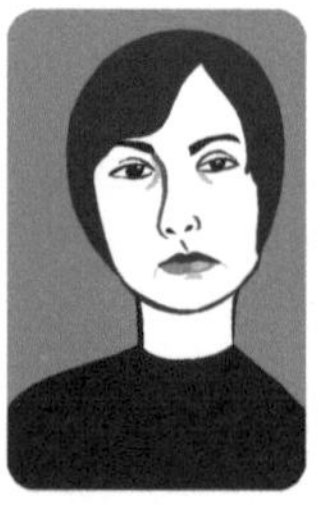

Julia Hartling

was born and raised in Tatarstan, Russia. After earning a PhD in evolutionary biology from Yale University, she returned to her childhood love of art and now works as a painter and illustrator in the Philadelphia area.
See more of Julia's work at www.juliahartling.com.

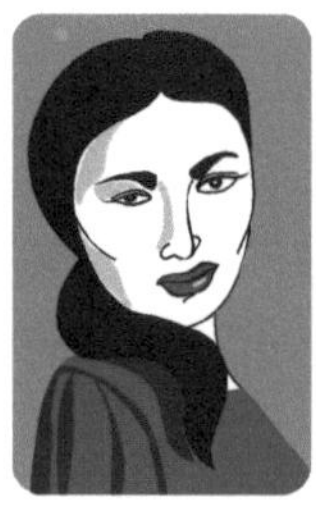

Melissa Markoff

holds a BA in Politics from Oberlin College. *Pluck This* is her first book.

Design by Jonathan Glick

www.ingramcontent.com/pod-product-compliance
Lightning Source LLC
LaVergne TN
LVHW070149110826
845147LV00002B/353

* 9 7 8 0 9 9 6 9 4 3 4 0 6 *